"Come dress yourself in love, let the journey begin."

-Francesca da Rimini

_____

_____

_____

_____

_____

_____

_____

_____

_____

_____

_____

_____

_____

_____

_____

_____

_____

_____

_____

_____

_____

_____

_____

_____

_____

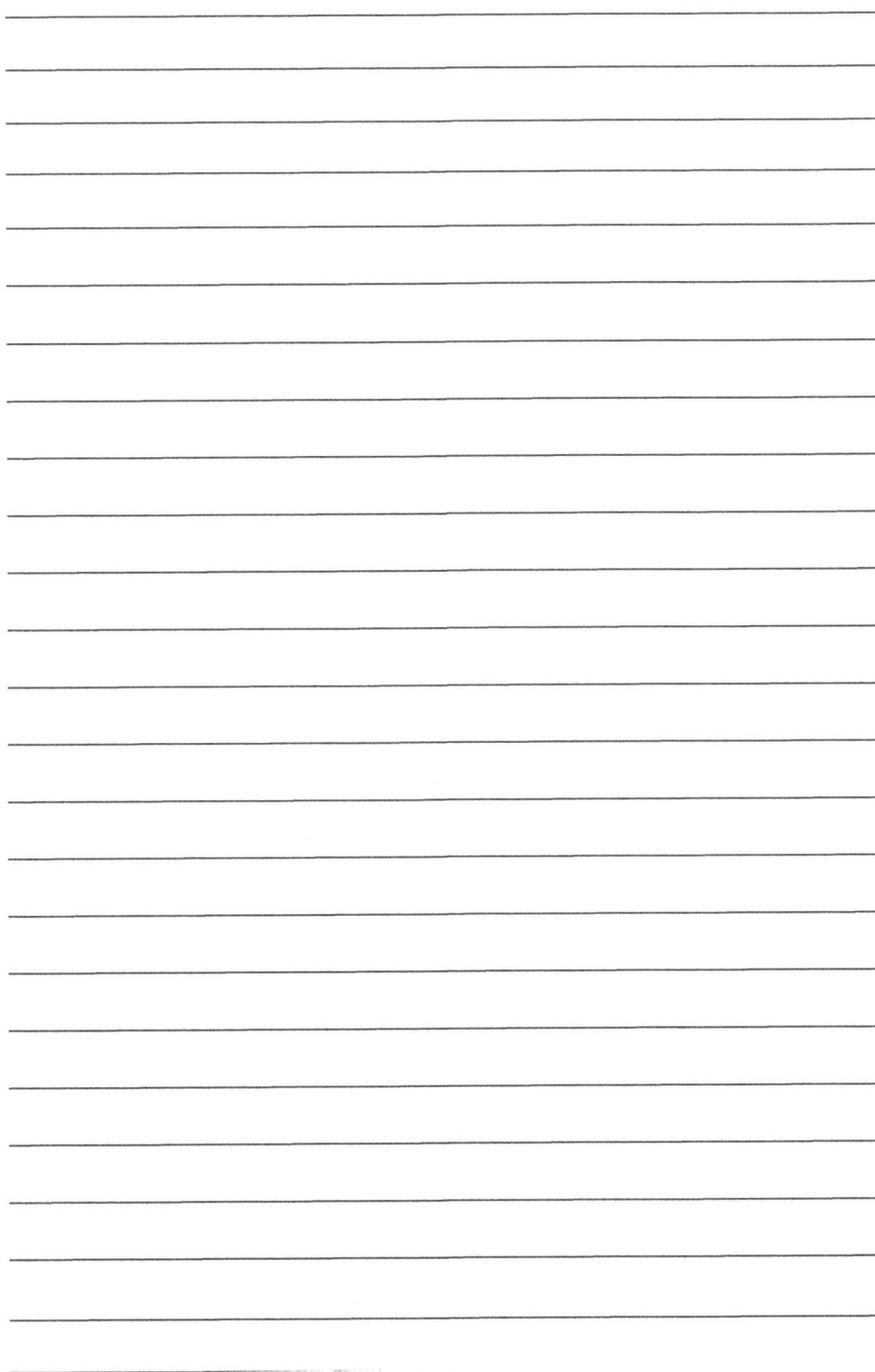

"Purpose is an essential element of you. Your very existence is wrapped up in the things you are here to fulfill."

-Chadwick Boseman

_____

_____

_____

_____

_____

_____

_____

_____

_____

_____

_____

_____

_____

_____

_____

_____

_____

_____

_____

_____

_____

_____

o————————o

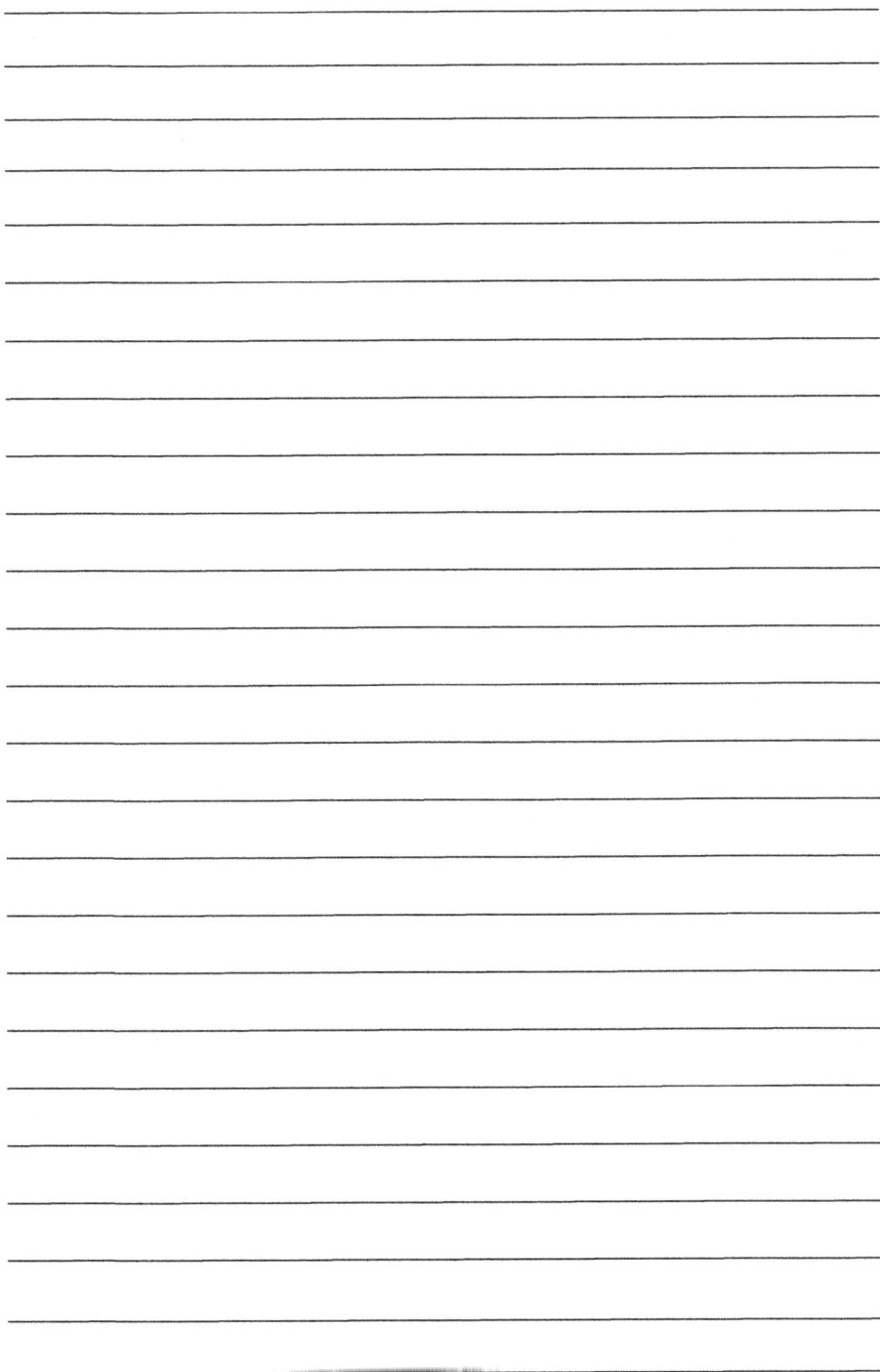

"Forever is composed of nows."

-Emily Dickenson

_____

_____

_____

_____

_____

_____

_____

_____

_____

_____

_____

_____

_____

_____

_____

_____

_____

_____

_____

_____

_____

_____

_____

_____

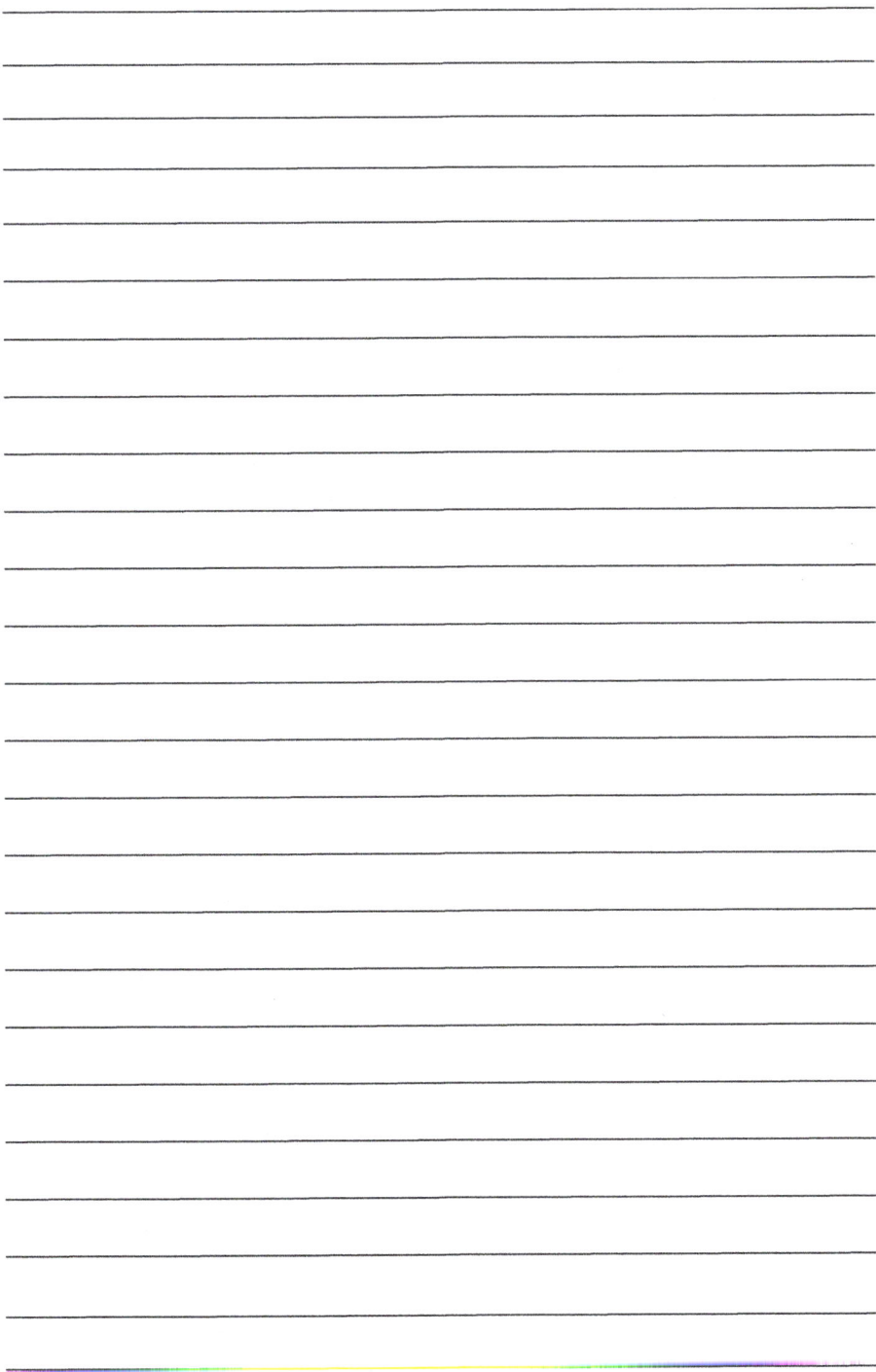

"How wonderful it is that nobody need wait a single moment before starting to improve the world."

-Anne Frank

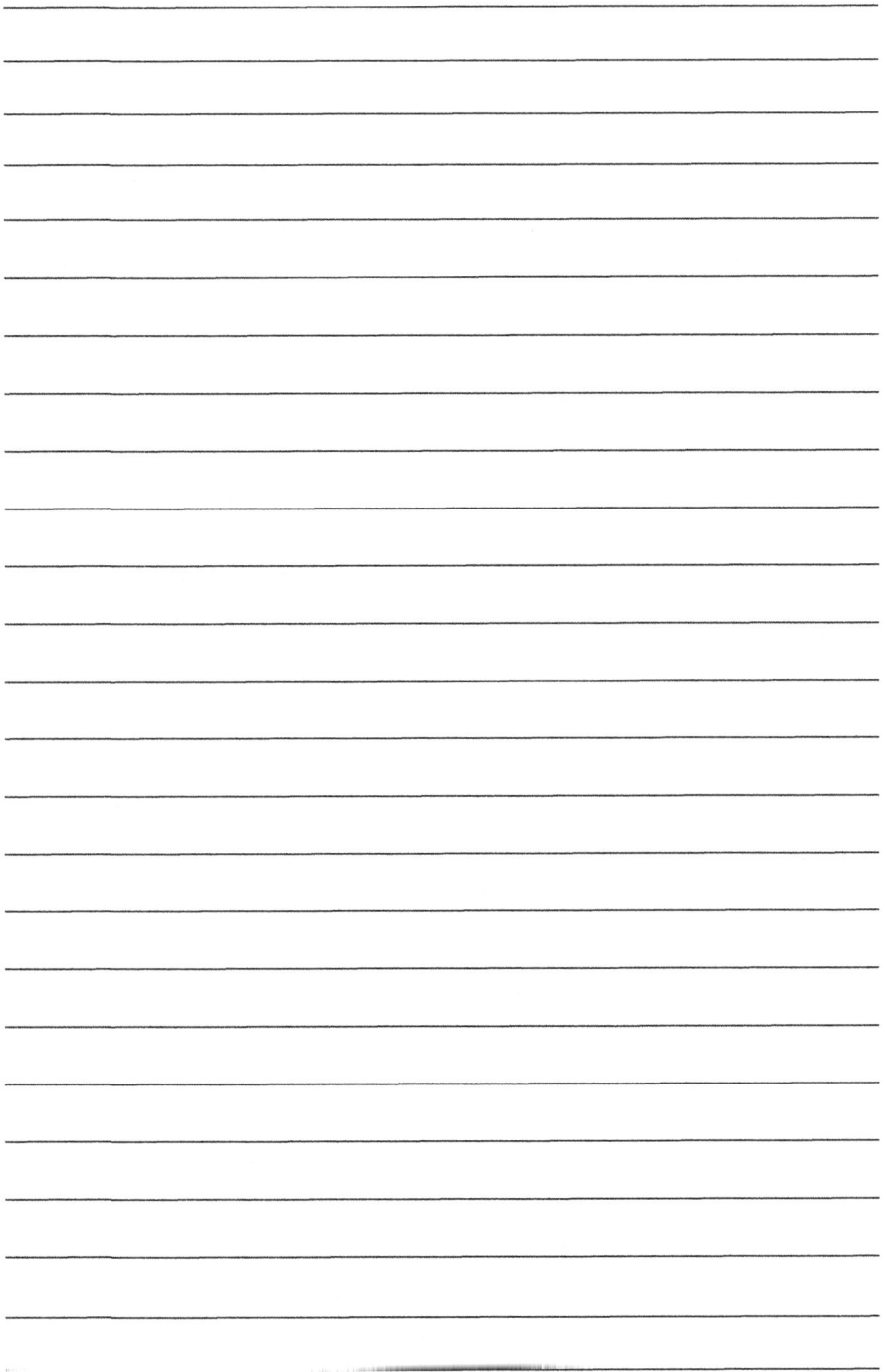

"Take care of the minutes, and the days will take care of themselves."
-Eliza Cook

"A journey of a thousand miles begins with a single step."

-Lao Tzu

"It is good to have an end to journey towards, but it is the journey that matters, in the end."

-Ursula Le Guin

"Success is a journey, not a destination. The doing is often more important than the outcome. "

-Arthur Ashe

"You cannot change your destination overnight, but you can change your direction overnight."

-Jim Rohn

_____

_____

_____

_____

_____

_____

_____

_____

_____

_____

_____

_____

_____

_____

_____

_____

_____

_____

_____

_____

_____

"Time is a created thing. To say, 'I don't have time' is like saying, 'I don't want to.'"

-Lao Tzu

"If all difficulties were known at the outset of a long journey, most of us would never start out at all."

-Dan Rather

"My destination is no longer a place, rather a new way of seeing."

-Marcel Proust

"The good life is a process, not a state of being. It is a direction, not a destination."

-Carl Rogers

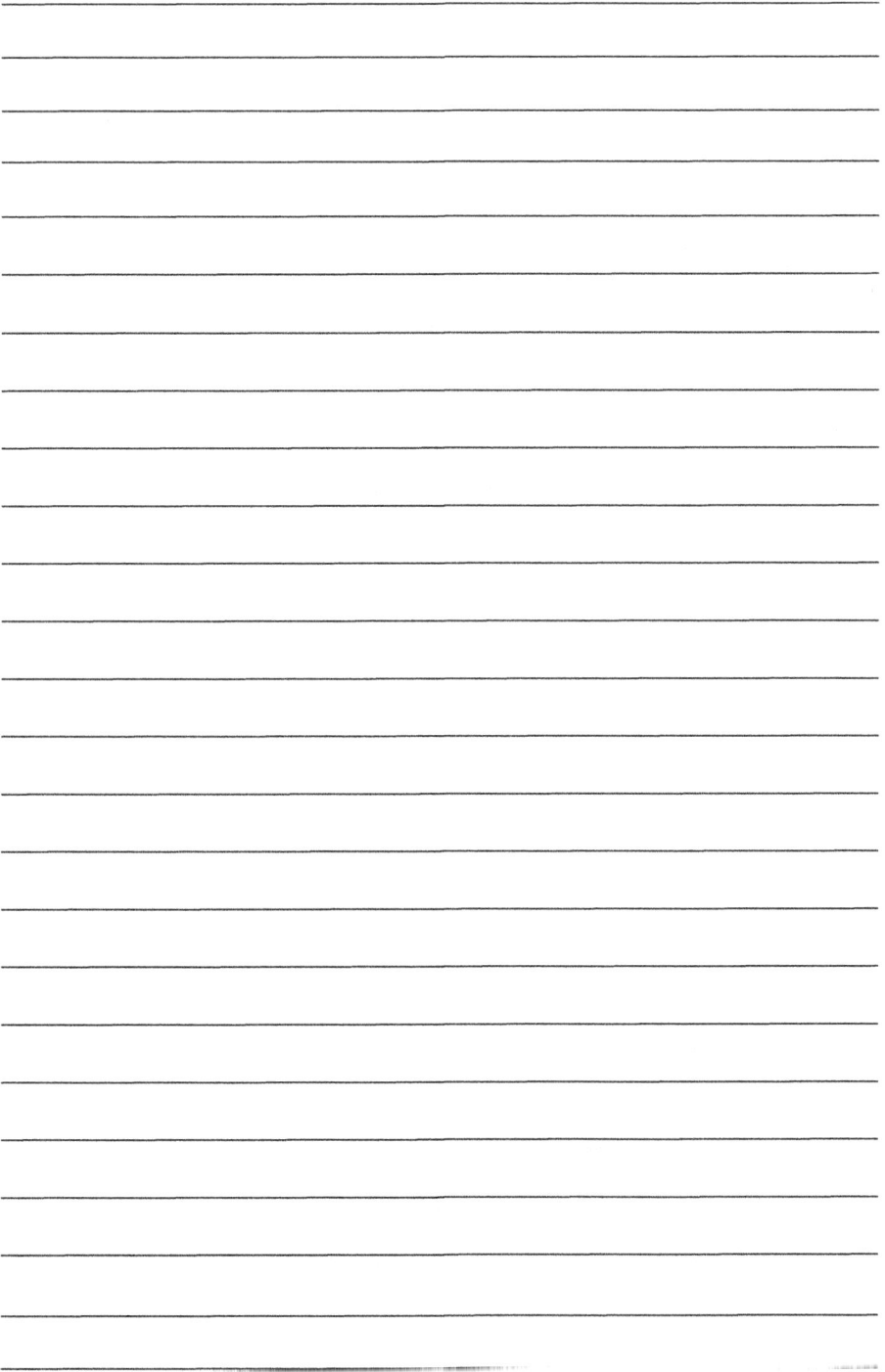

"Love recognizes no barriers. It jumps hurdles, leaps fences, penetrates walls to arrive at its destination full of hope."

- Maya Angelou

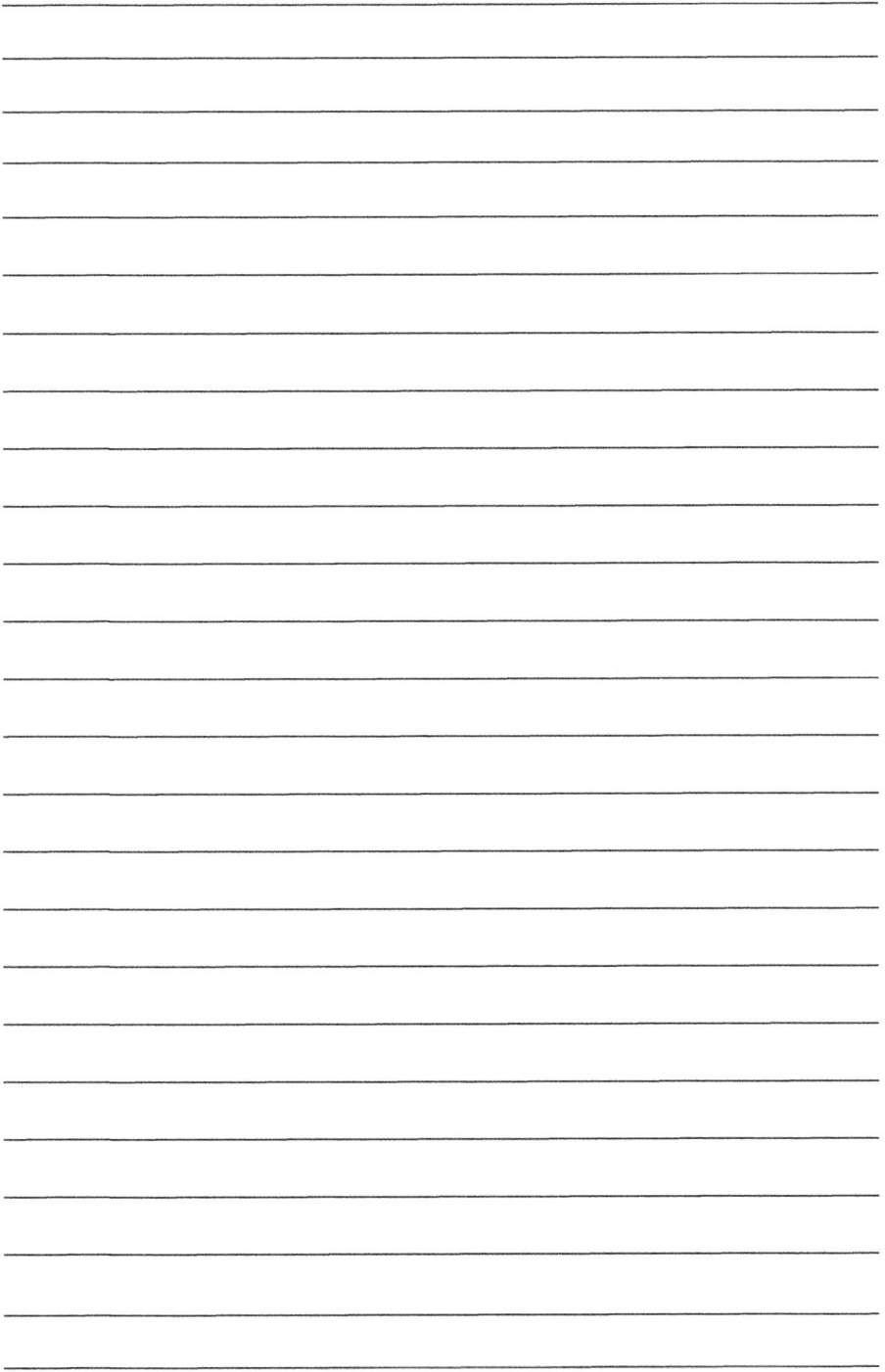

"Success is not a destination, but the road. Being successful means that you're working hard and walking your walk every day."

- Marlon Wayans

"What keeps you going isn't some final destination but the road you're on, and the fact that you know how to drive."

- Barbara Kingsolver

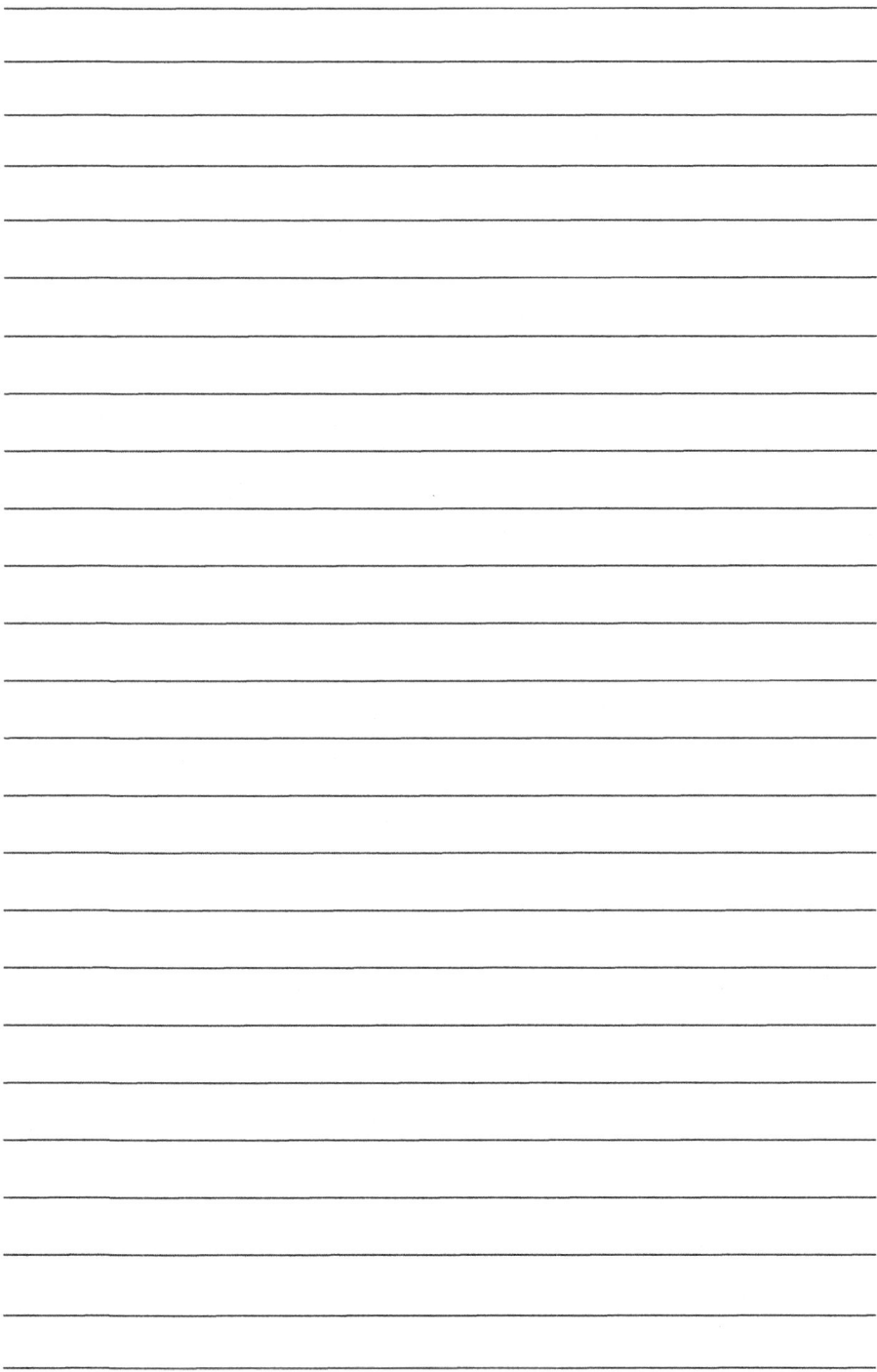

"All journeys have secret destinations of which the traveler is unaware."
- Martin Buber

"You will never reach your destination if you stop and throw stones at every dog that barks."

- Winston Churchill

_____

_____

_____

_____

_____

_____

_____

_____

_____

_____

_____

_____

_____

_____

_____

_____

_____

_____

_____

_____

_____

_____

o——————————o

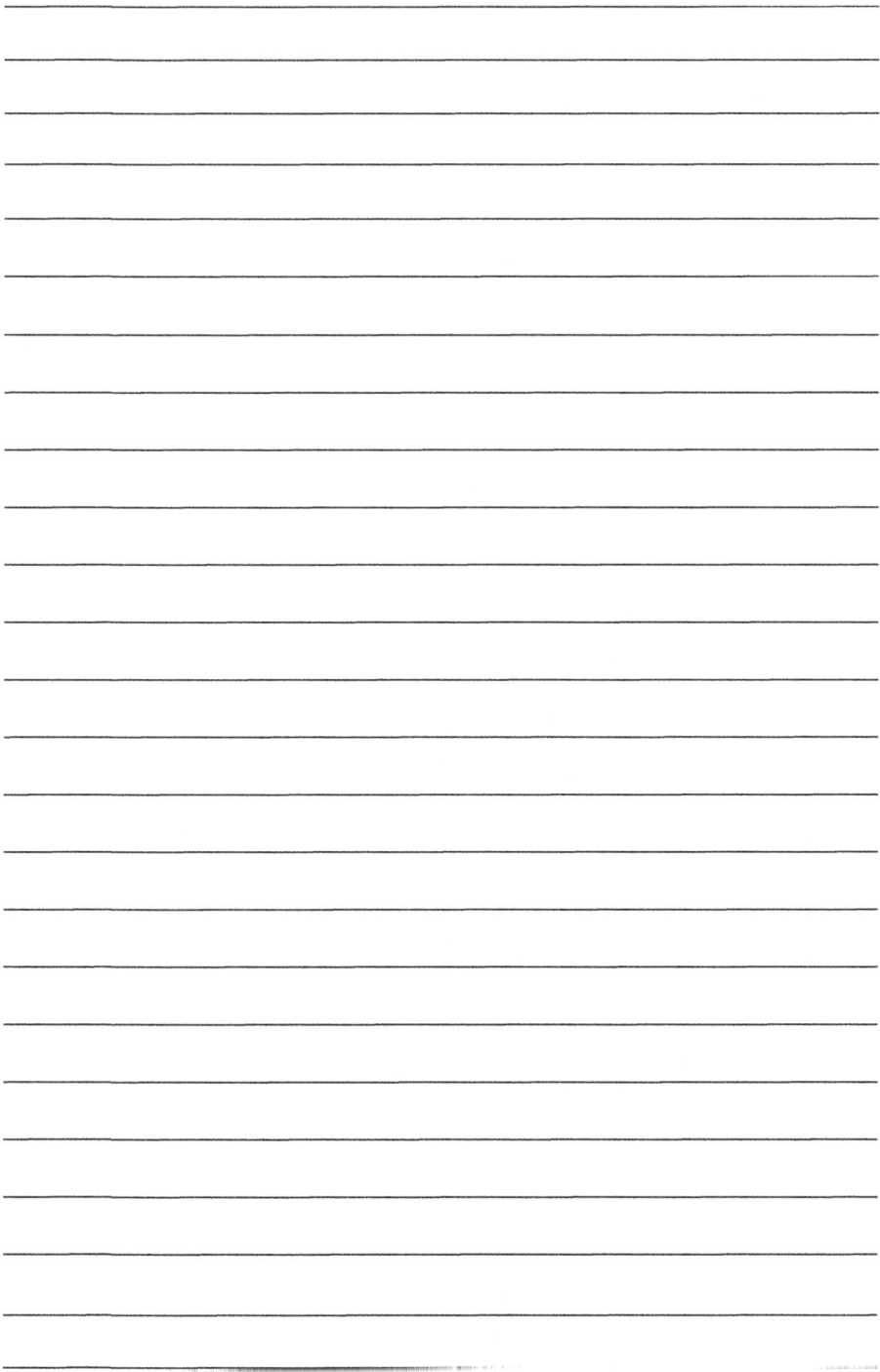

"We shall not cease from exploration, and the end of all our exploring will be to arrive where we started and know the place for the first time."

- T. S. Eliot

"The ship is always off course. Anybody who sails knows that. Sailing is being off course and correcting. That gives a sense of what life is about."

-Michael Meade

_____

_____

_____

_____

_____

_____

_____

_____

_____

_____

_____

_____

_____

_____

_____

_____

_____

_____

_____

_____

_____

_____

o────────o

"Find the courage to ask yourself the questions you're afraid to hear the answer to? Why... Because it's the only way you'll know which direction your truth lays."
-Nikki Rowe

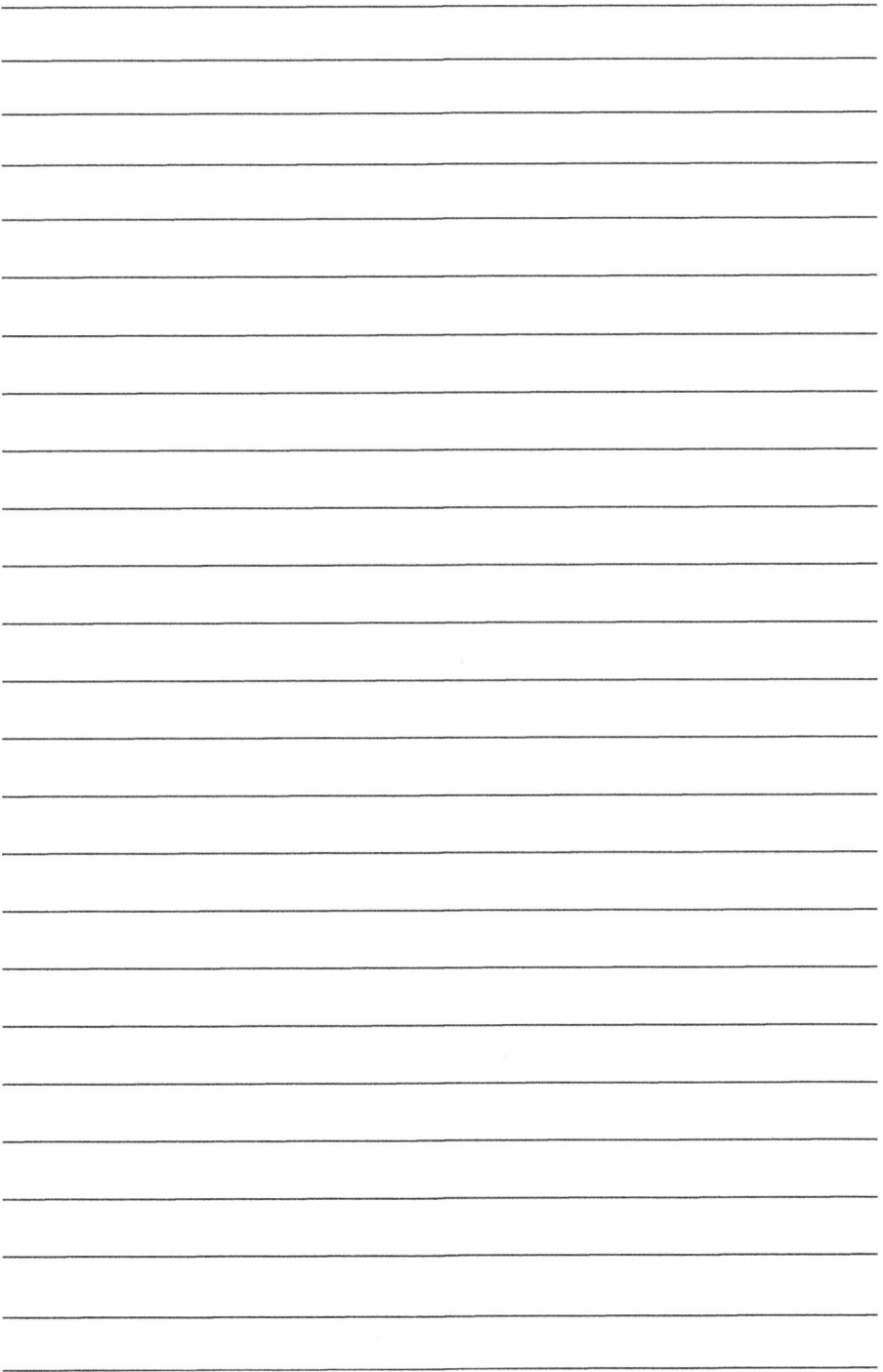

"Life is the journey of coming home to ourselves."

— Lisa Cypers Kamen

_____

_____

_____

_____

_____

_____

_____

_____

_____

_____

_____

_____

_____

_____

_____

_____

_____

_____

_____

_____

_____

_____

_____

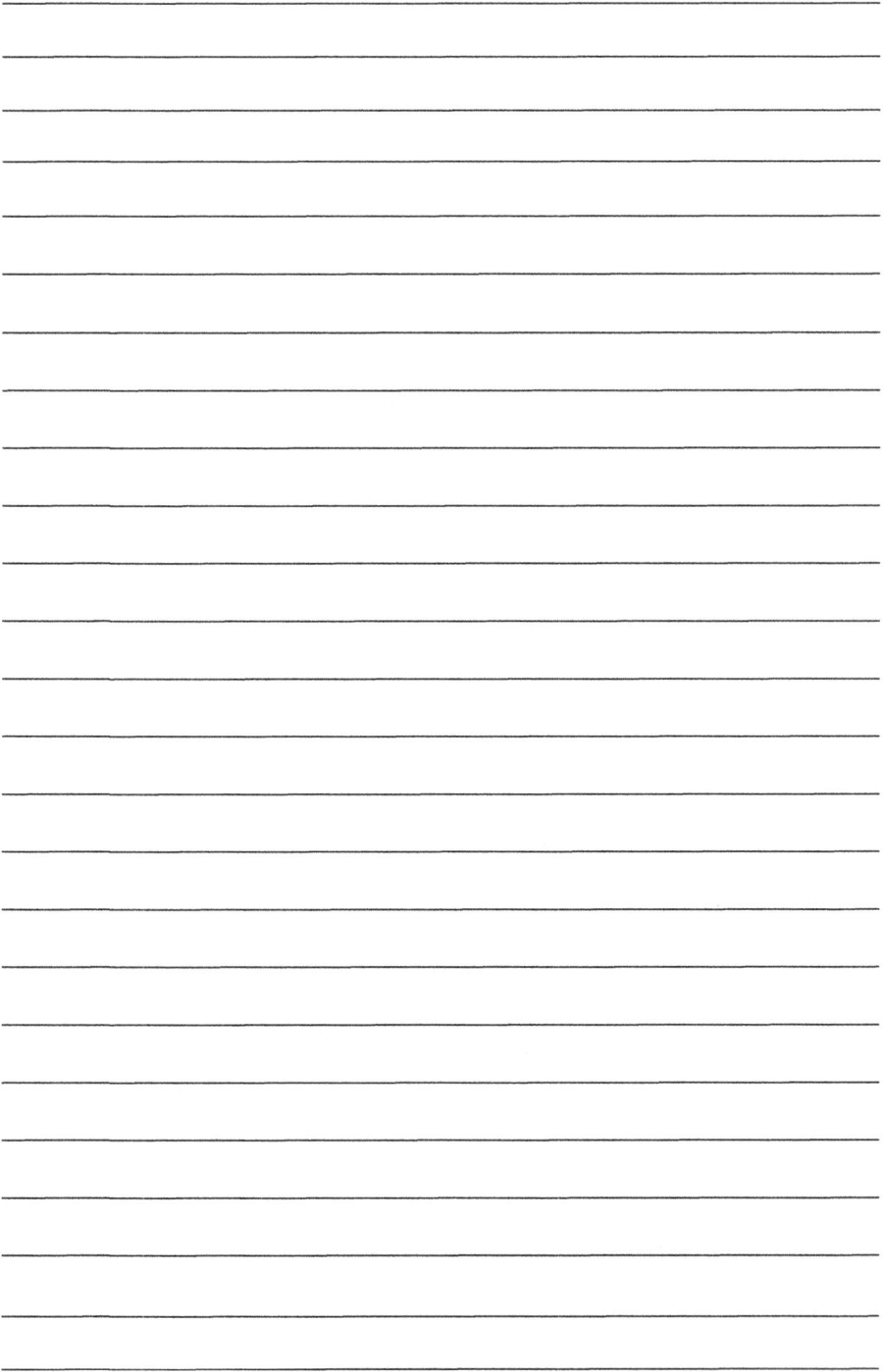

The journey will undoubtedly be a winding one, filled with surprises and setbacks. But I'm ready to embrace it fully, wherever it may take me."

-Mallika Chopra

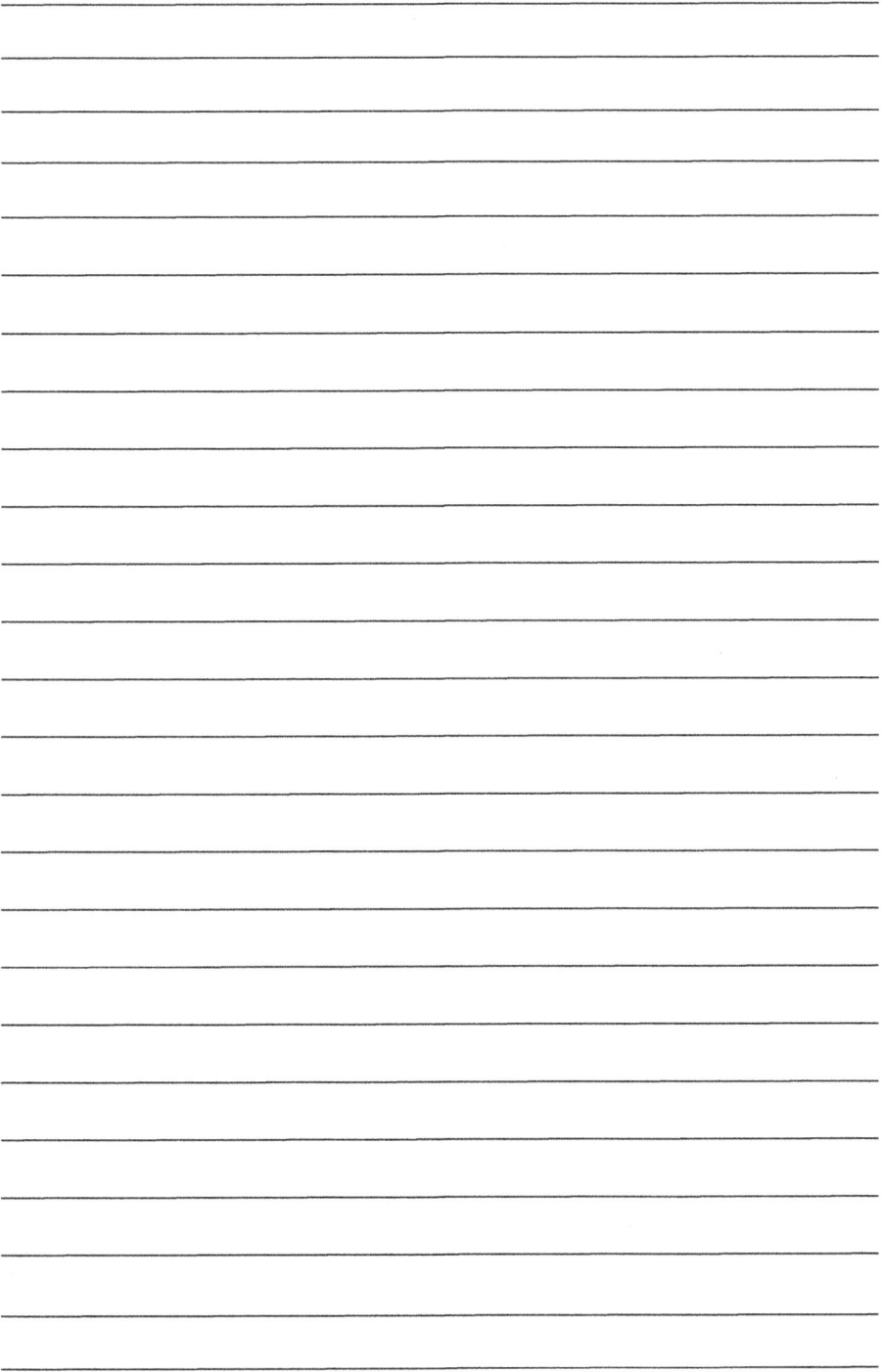

"I must give you this warning: your journeys will rarely ever go as you plan. You will make mistakes, and you will feel lost. Whenever that happens, look to the light and keep moving forward in faith." -Seth Adams Smith

"If it was all about the destination, we'd spend our nights sleeping in graves."

-Karishma Magvani

_____

_____

_____

_____

_____

_____

_____

_____

_____

_____

_____

_____

_____

_____

_____

_____

_____

_____

_____

_____

o——————o

"Being kind, being compassionate, being respectful does not make you weak. More often, it's the harder path to take."

-Liza M. Wiemer

_____

_____

_____

_____

_____

_____

_____

_____

_____

_____

_____

_____

_____

_____

_____

_____

_____

_____

_____

_____

_____

_____

_____

_____

"Passion is what makes us amazing, however, finding your passion is one thing, following it is another. Through both journeys, please, do not feed the fears."

-Efrat Cybulkiewicz

_____

_____

_____

_____

_____

_____

_____

_____

_____

_____

_____

_____

_____

_____

_____

_____

_____

_____

_____

_____

_____

_____

_____

○———————○

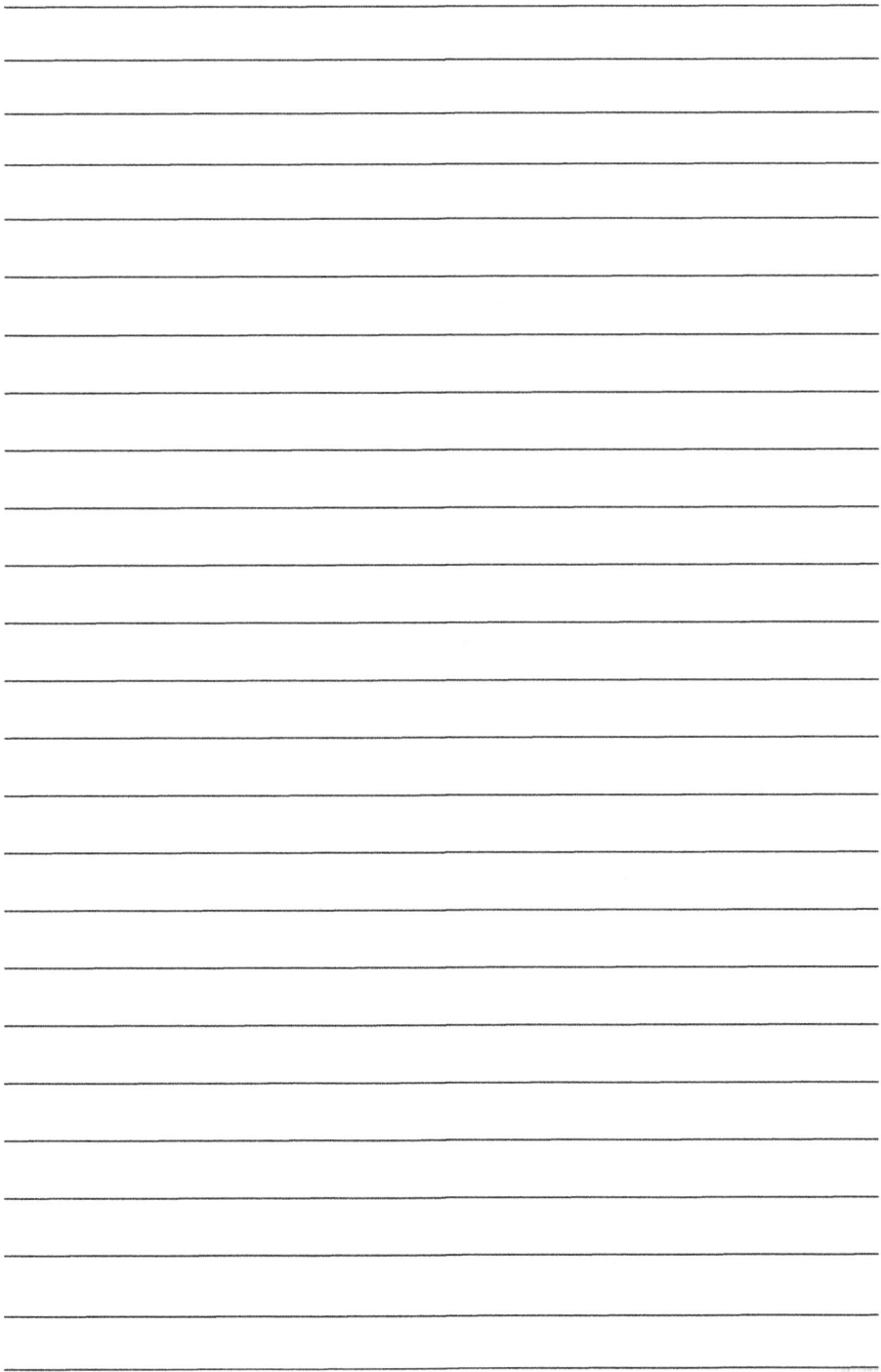

"It is better to travel on the rough right road than the smooth wrong way."
-Lailah Gifty Akita

_____

_____

_____

_____

_____

_____

_____

_____

_____

_____

_____

_____

_____

_____

_____

_____

_____

_____

_____

_____

_____

_____

_____

_____

_____

o———————o

"Take time for the clearance of the mind, preparing for adherence to perseverance for the journey of another thousand miles."

-Curtis Tyrone Jones

"Sometimes the only way to find the answers, is not to travel far away, but to venture deeper within ourselves."

-Mimi Novic

_____

_____

_____

_____

_____

_____

_____

_____

_____

_____

_____

_____

_____

_____

_____

_____

_____

_____

_____

_____

o———————o

"Everywhere you go, you shall find dramatic splendor and awe because your majestic soul is part of the vivid whole, and nothing about you is ignoble."

-Kilroy J. Oldster

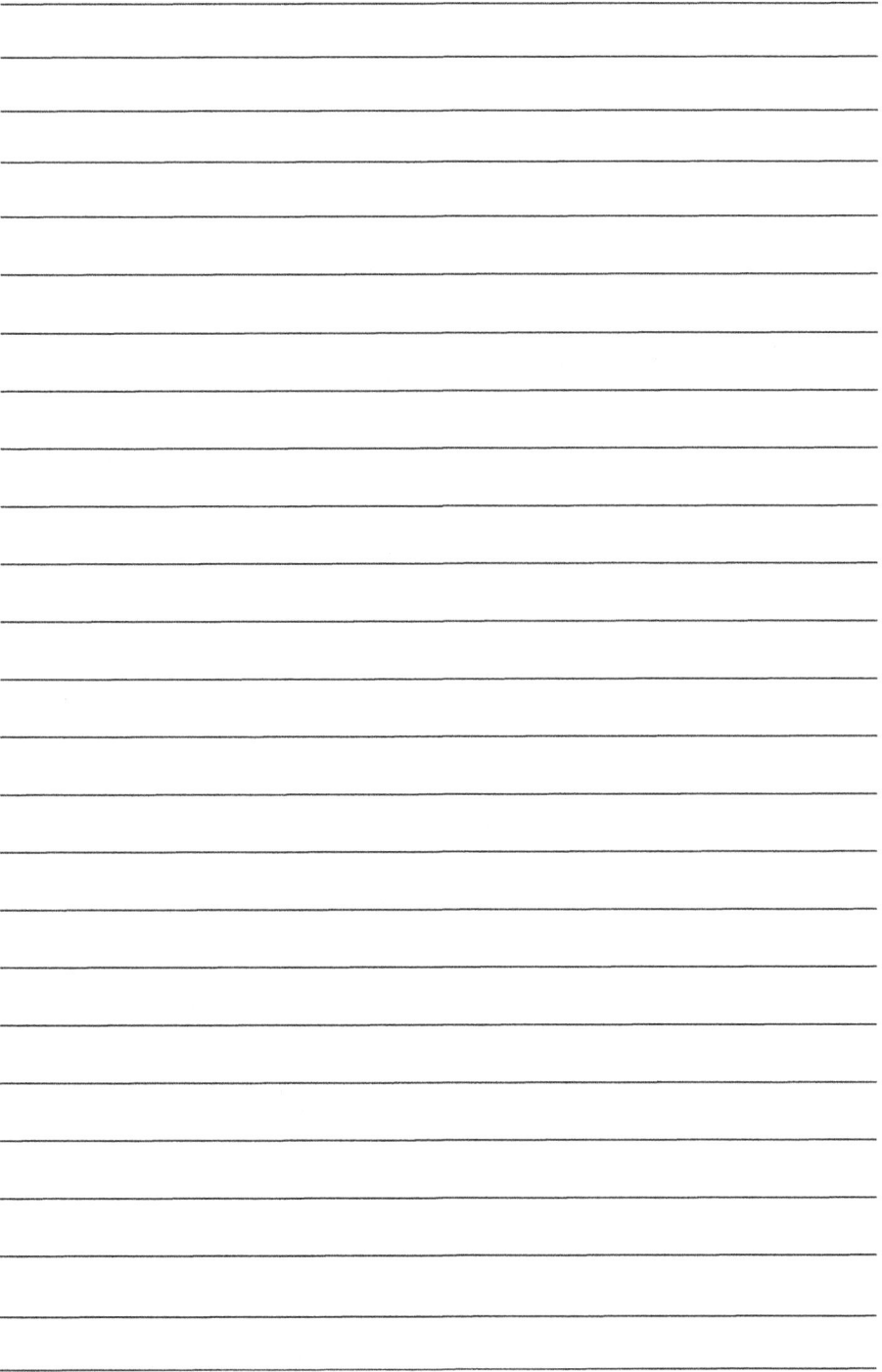

"The goal of my life is to tie adventure to my feet, stock memories in my pocket, hold imagination in my palms like fairy dust and sprinkle it on my tales."

-Mitali Meelan

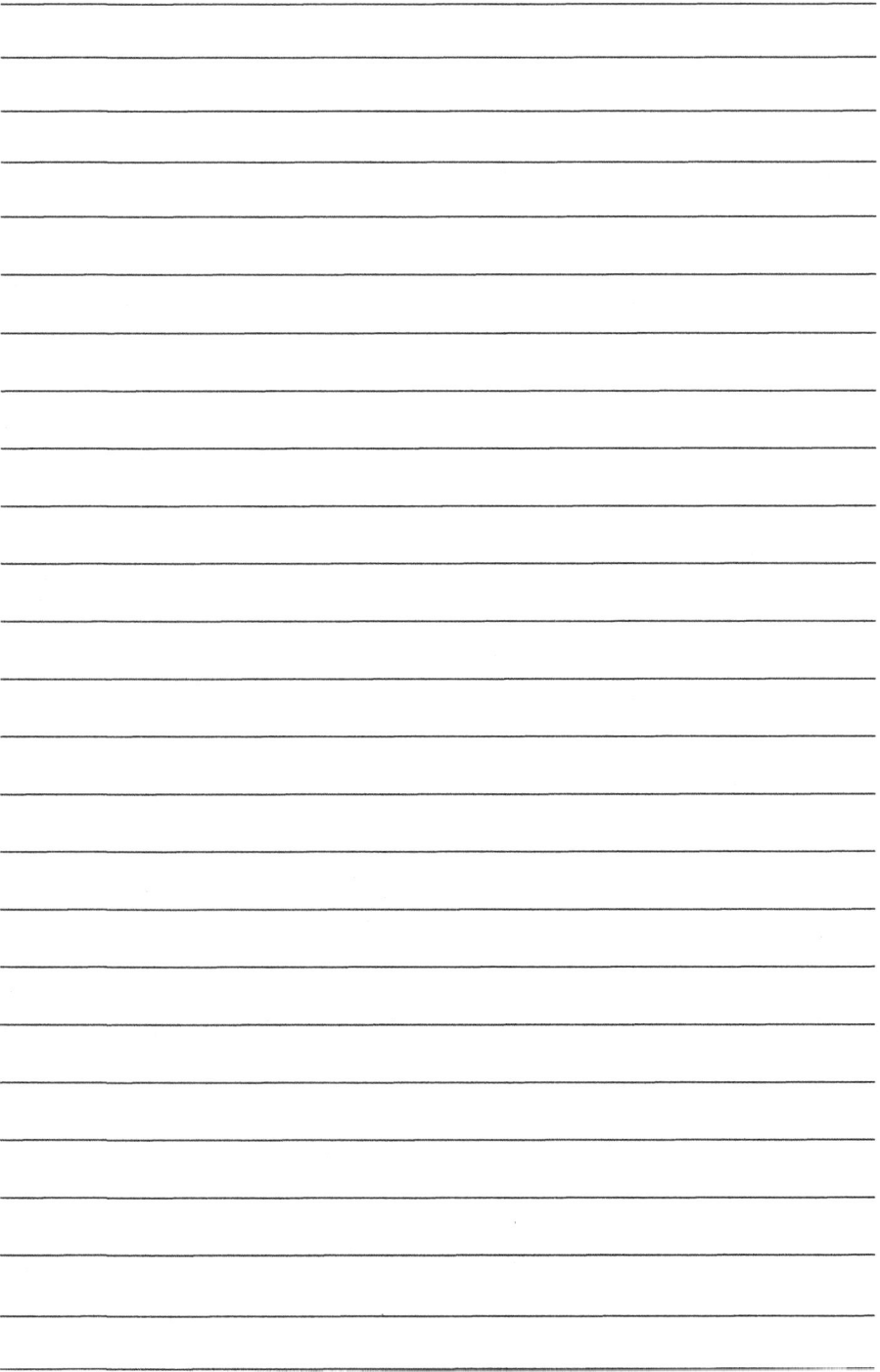

"You're on the path and have already begun to morph - so has the road.
The journey has chosen you. The only way out is forward and through."

-Helen S. Rosenau

"Your life is your own unique journey -- it is unlike a journey any other person, before you or after you, will ever take."

-Shon Mehta

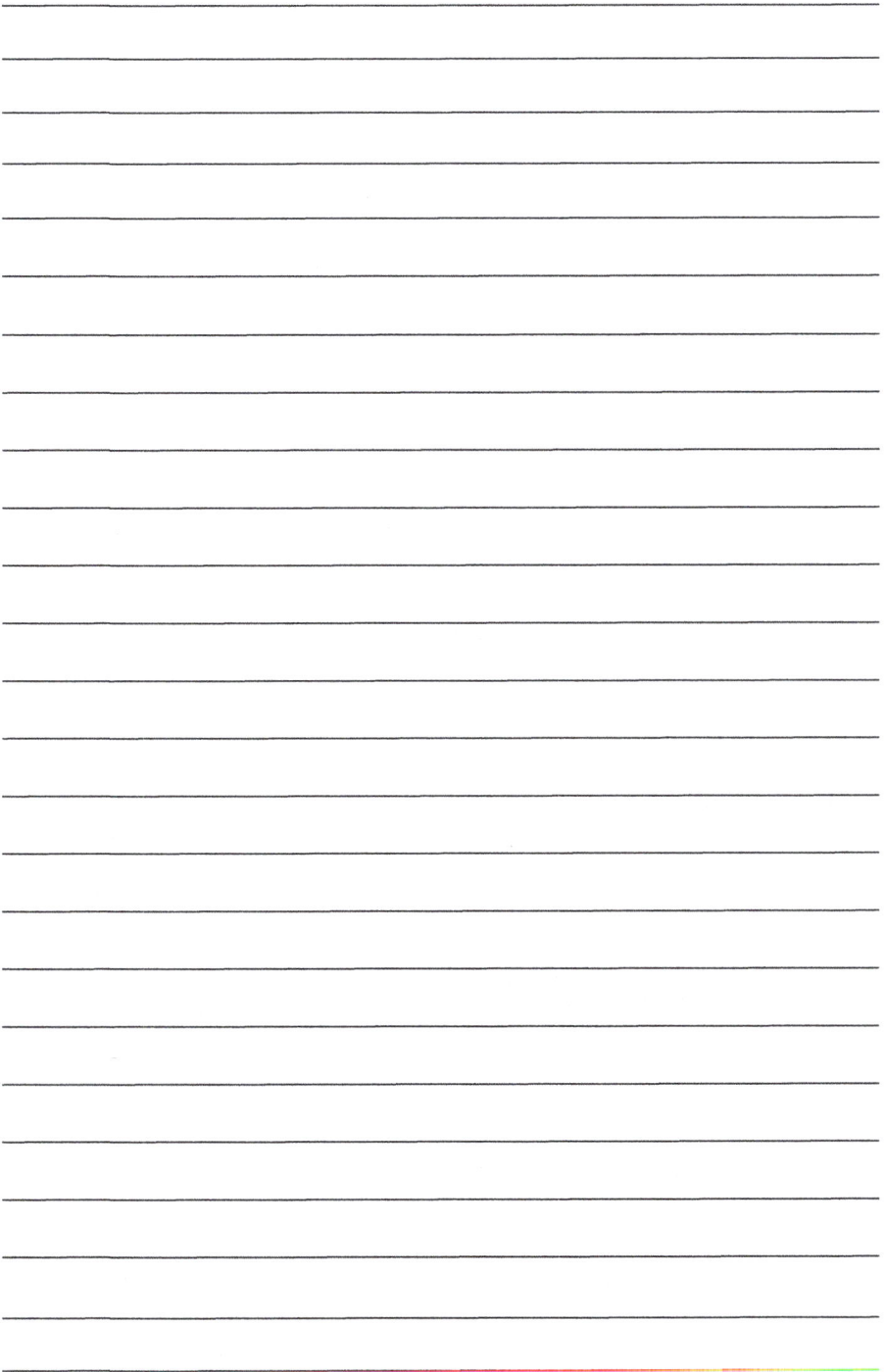

"If I'm not certain where I'm at and if I've not quite determined where I want to go, I'll eventually find myself in neither place."

-Craig D. Lounsbrough

_____

_____

_____

_____

_____

_____

_____

_____

_____

_____

_____

_____

_____

_____

_____

_____

_____

_____

_____

_____

_____

_____

o———————————o

"The remarkable journey of a person lies in his visions and not a followed path of anyone else."

-Aayush Verma

"No one can save a person from his or her thoughts and deeds except oneself. We make the choices that become our destiny."

-Kilroy J. Oldster

"When planning life's journey, always have an alternate route."

-Frank Sonnenberg

---

o———————o

"And at the end of the day, there is nothing but the journey. Because destination is pure illusion."

-Rich Roll

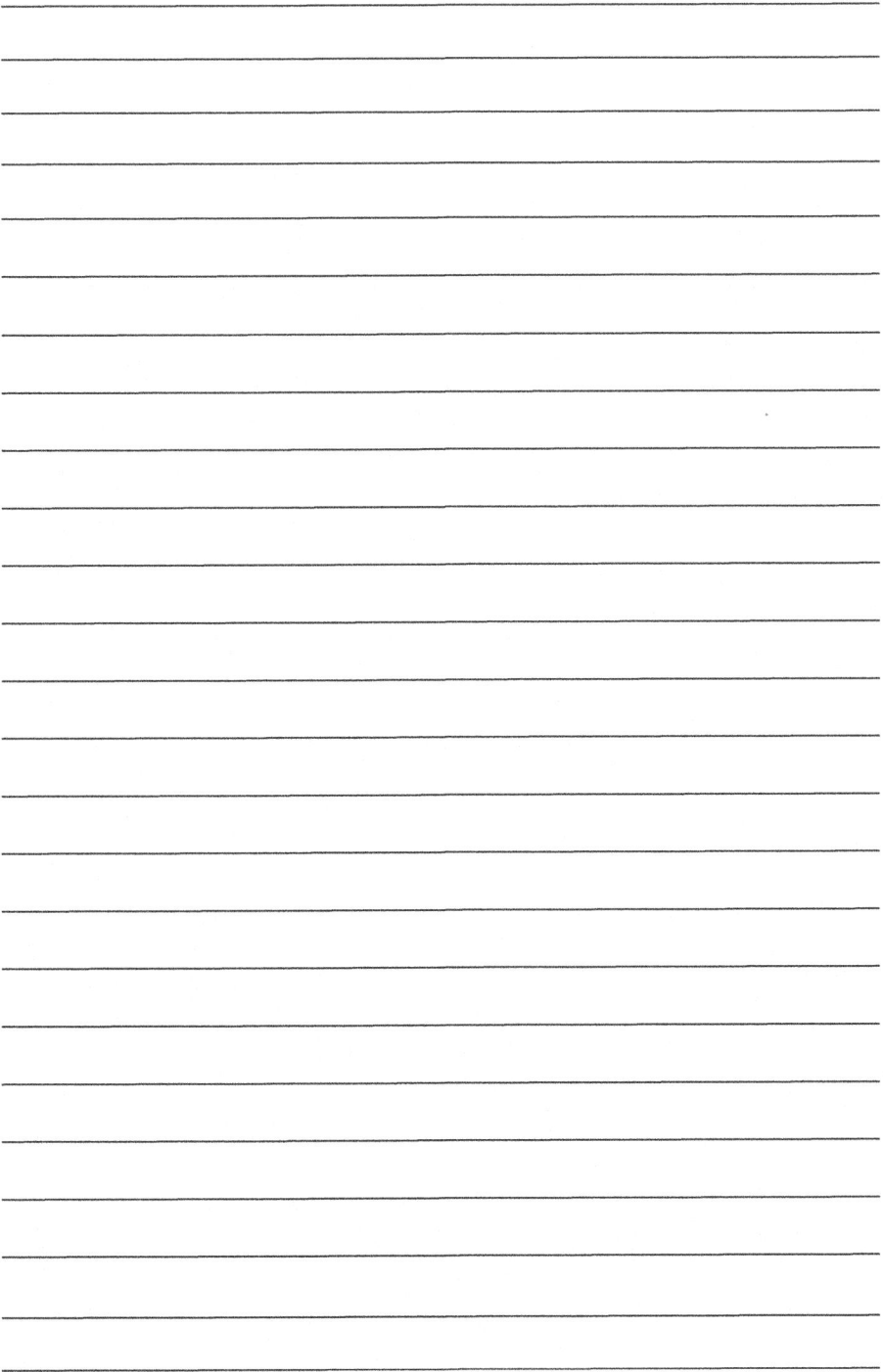

"There is a bend in the road. I don't know what lies around that bend, but I hope for the best."

-Lucy Maud Montgomery

_____

_____

_____

_____

_____

_____

_____

_____

_____

_____

_____

_____

_____

_____

_____

_____

_____

_____

_____

_____

_____

_____

_____

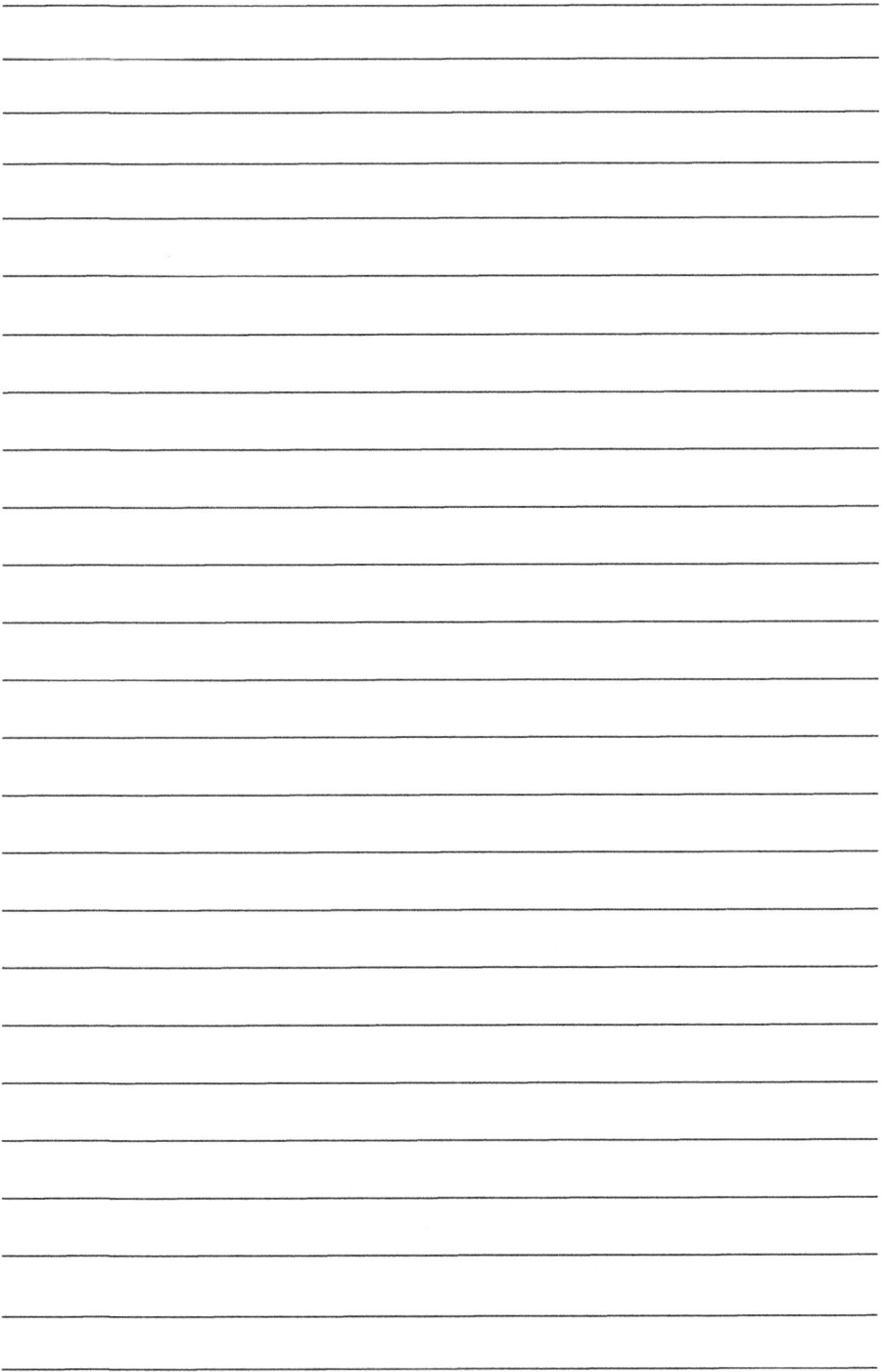

"The only way we will love our neighbor as ourselves is by getting to know our neighbors, even in the midst of our differences."

-Eric Overby

"The journey to a peaceful and blessed life begins when you take 100 percent responsibility for your life instead of blaming others."

-Nitin Namdeo

"Wherever you go, go with the wholeness of your heart."

-Lailah Gifty Akita

"Life is a staircase where we can only recall about steps backward but we only have to reach forward."

-Srinivas Mishra

"There are beautiful places everywhere; we just have to travel with a beautiful heart."

-Bhuwan Thapaliya

_____

_____

_____

_____

_____

_____

_____

_____

_____

_____

_____

_____

_____

_____

_____

_____

_____

_____

_____

_____

_____

_____

_____

"Travel down that road far enough and you forget entirely where you came from. The journey becomes the destination in a twisted sort of way."

-Terry Brooks

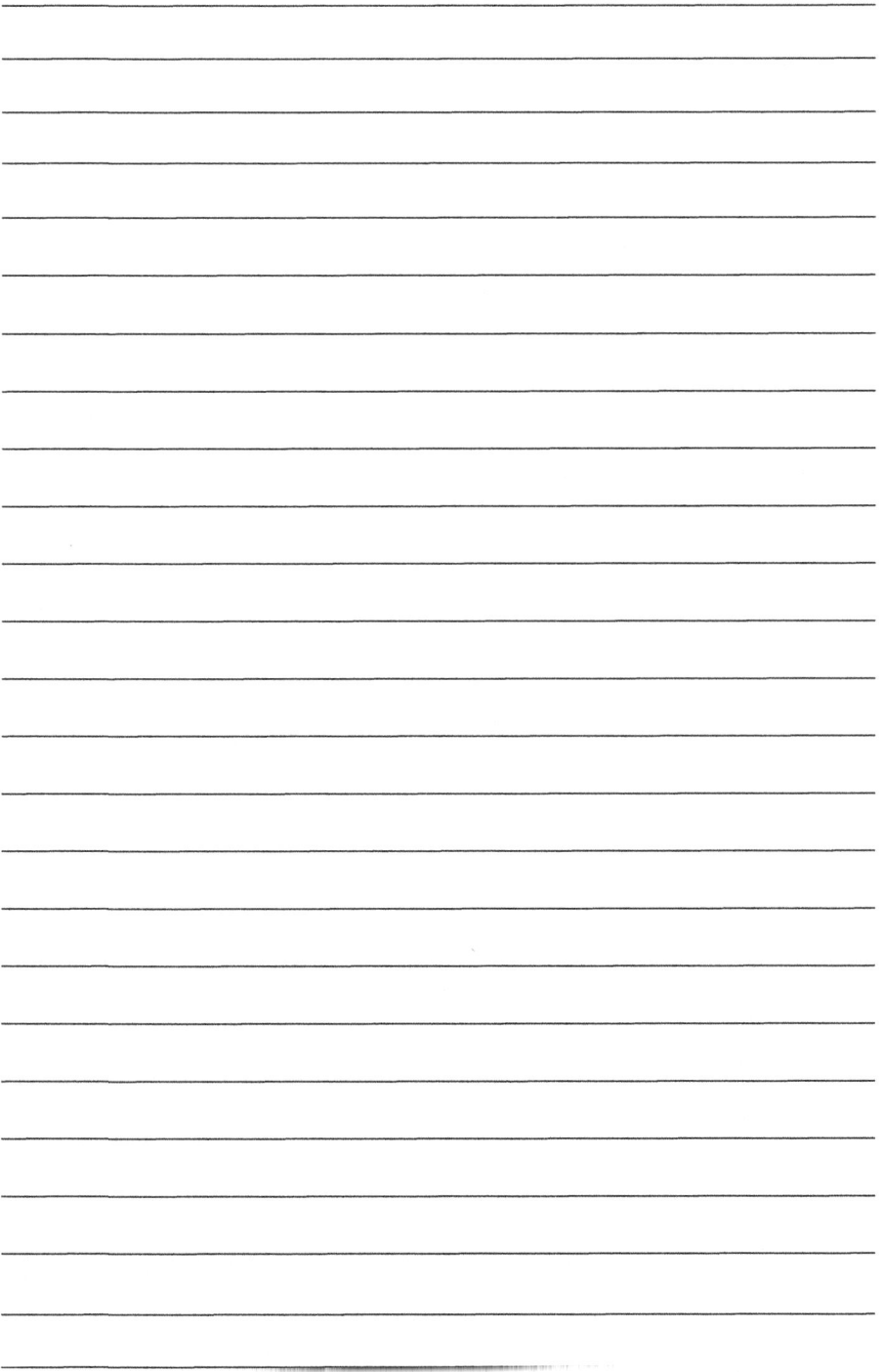

"Delays and disappointments are often only detours along the journey of life."

-Amelia Rose

_____

_____

_____

_____

_____

_____

_____

_____

_____

_____

_____

_____

_____

_____

_____

_____

_____

_____

_____

_____

_____

_____

o———————o

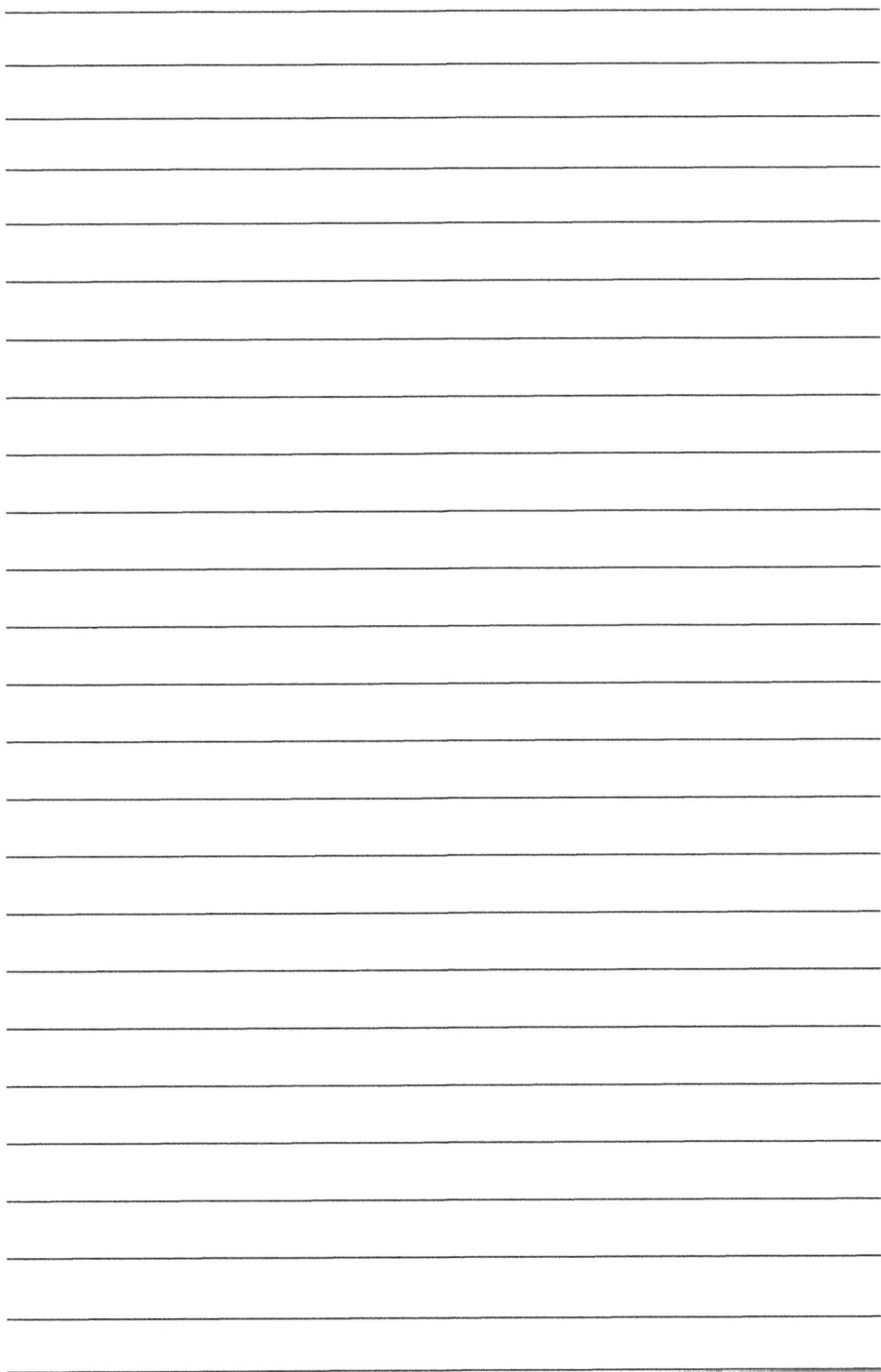

"Never be afraid to travel on a new path."

-Lailah Gifty Akita

"Life has a tendency to provide a person with what they need in order to grow."

-Kilroy J. Oldster

_____

_____

_____

_____

_____

_____

_____

_____

_____

_____

_____

_____

_____

_____

_____

_____

_____

_____

_____

_____

_____

_____

_____

o———————o

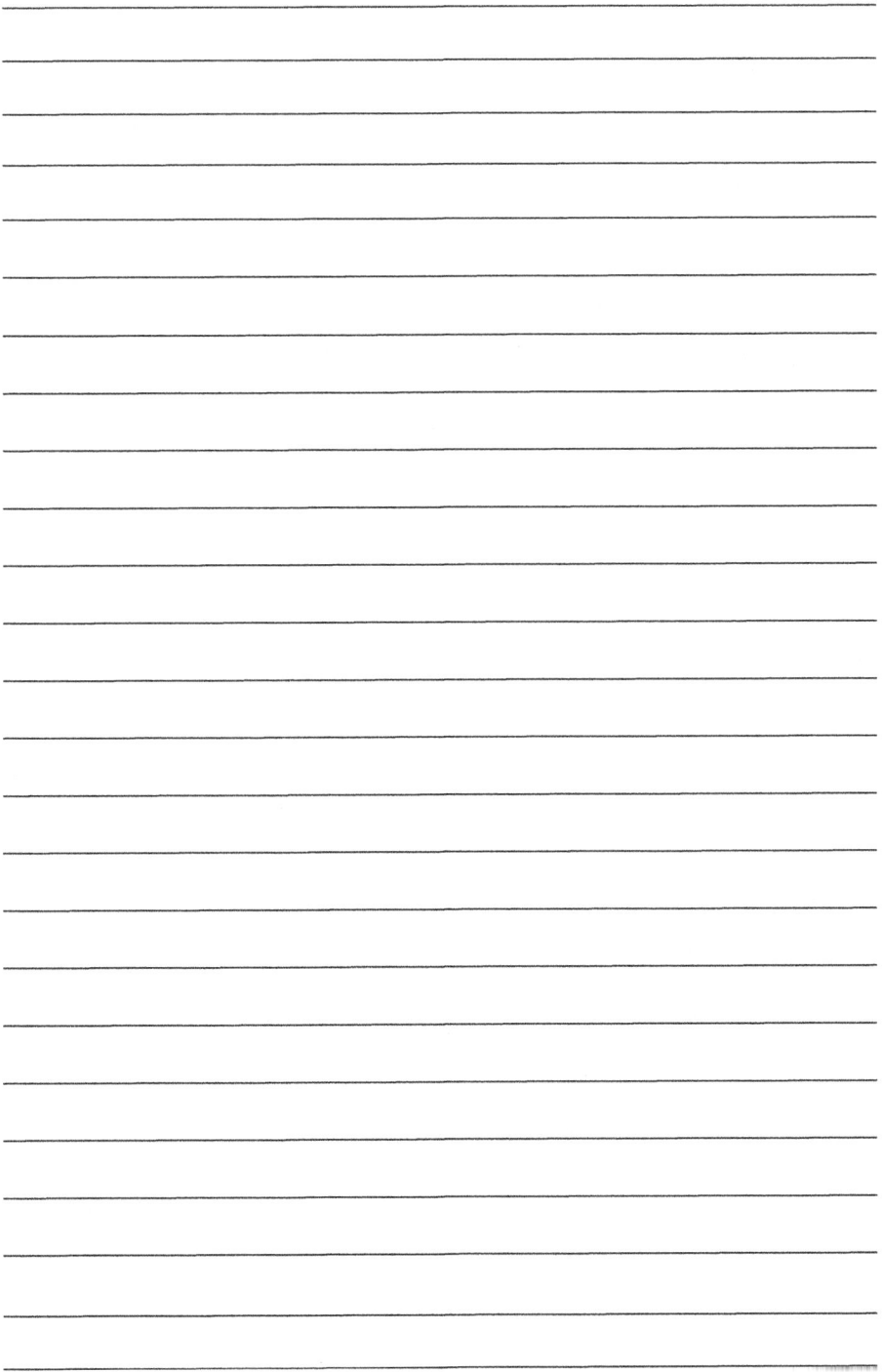

"You'll learn, as you get older, that rules are made to be broken. Be bold enough to live life on your terms, and never, ever apologize for it."

-Mandy Hale

_____

_____

_____

_____

_____

_____

_____

_____

_____

_____

_____

_____

_____

_____

_____

_____

_____

_____

_____

_____

_____

_____

"For my part, I travel not to go anywhere, but to go. I travel for travel's sake. The great affair is to move."

-Robert Louis Stevenson

_____

_____

_____

_____

_____

_____

_____

_____

_____

_____

_____

_____

_____

_____

_____

_____

_____

_____

_____

_____

_____

_____

_____

"The only impossible journey is the one you never begin."

-Tony Robbins

_____

_____

_____

_____

_____

_____

_____

_____

_____

_____

_____

_____

_____

_____

_____

_____

_____

_____

_____

_____

_____

_____

_____

_____

o————————o

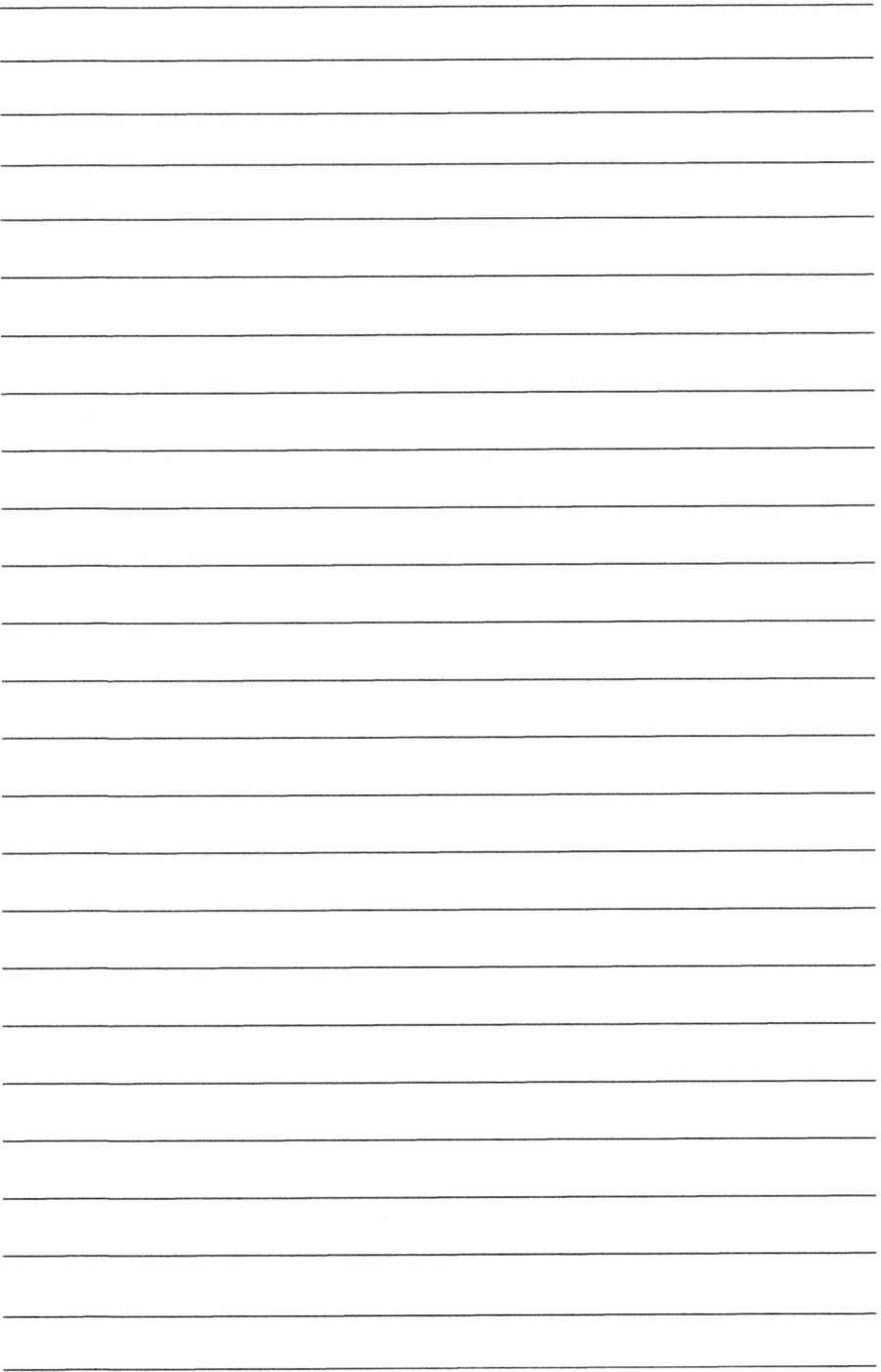

"People don't take trips, trips take people."

-John Steinbeck

_____

_____

_____

_____

_____

_____

_____

_____

_____

_____

_____

_____

_____

_____

_____

_____

_____

_____

_____

_____

_____

_____

_____

_____

o————————o

"Everything I was I carry with me, everything I will be lies waiting on the road ahead."

-Ma Jian

"Once you have traveled, the voyage never ends, but is played out over and over again in the quietest chambers. The mind can never break off from the journey."

-Pat Conroy

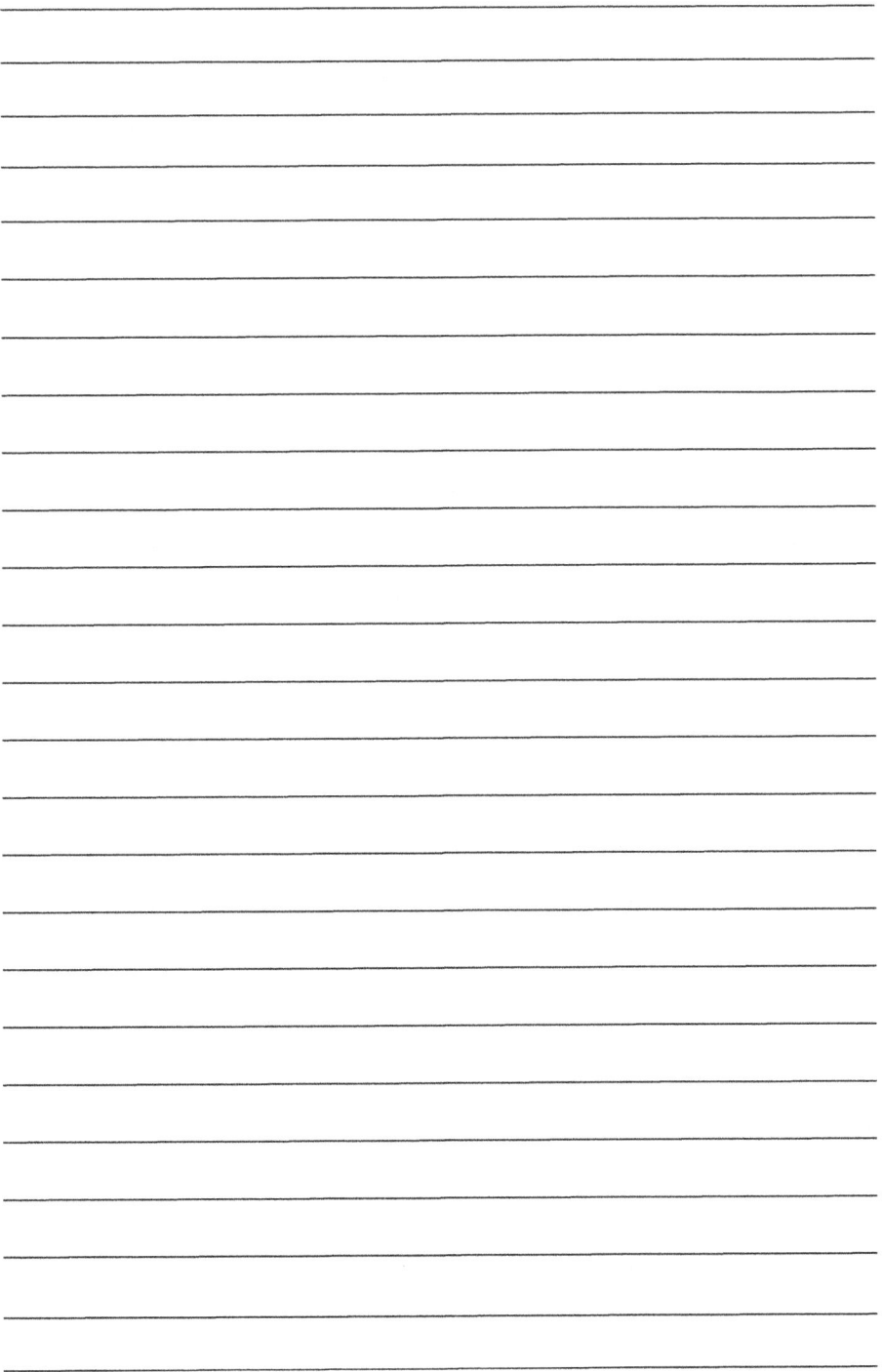

"Some beautiful paths can't be discovered without getting lost."

- Erol Ozan

"Make voyages. Attempt them. There's nothing else."

-Tennessee Williams

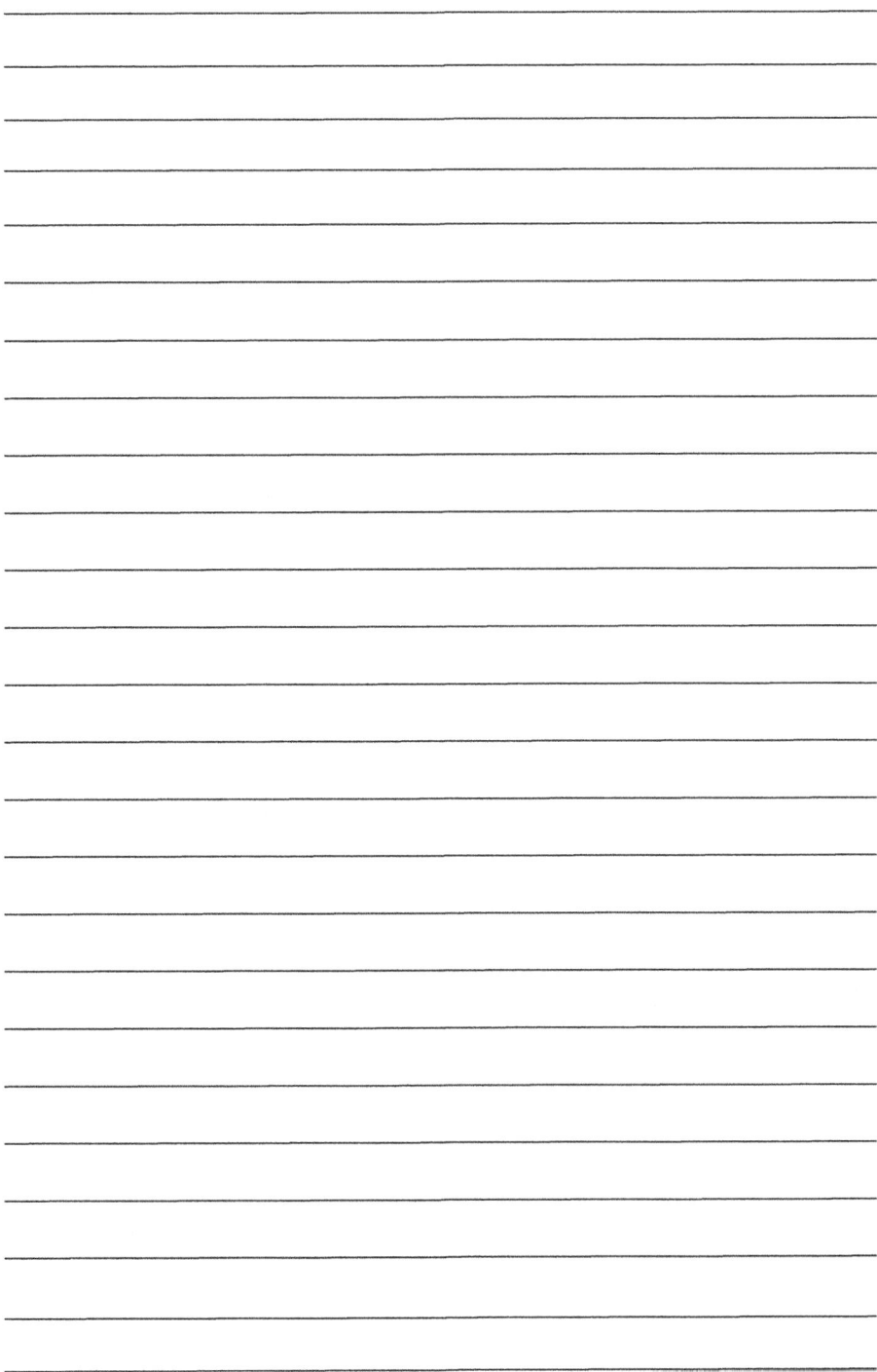

"It is not the destination where you end up but the mishaps and memories you create along the way."

-Penelope Riley

"Life is pure adventure, and the sooner we realize that, the sooner we will be able to treat life as art."

-Maya Angelou

"To live the greatest number of good hours is wisdom."

-Ralph Waldo Emerson

_____

_____

_____

_____

_____

_____

_____

_____

_____

_____

_____

_____

_____

_____

_____

_____

_____

_____

_____

_____

_____

_____

_____

_____

o———————o

"The woods are lovely, dark and deep. But I have promises to keep, and miles to go before I sleep."

-Robert Frost

"It is confidence in our bodies, minds and spirits that allows us to keep looking for new adventures and new lessons to learn."

-Oprah Winfrey

_____

_____

_____

_____

_____

_____

_____

_____

_____

_____

_____

_____

_____

_____

_____

_____

_____

_____

_____

_____

_____

_____

_____

_____

_____

o———————o

"But there is also a restlessness about nature that resonates with our own lives – always thrusting ahead, exploring new forms as it evolves."

-Adam Ford

"Travel far enough, you meet yourself."

-David Mitchel

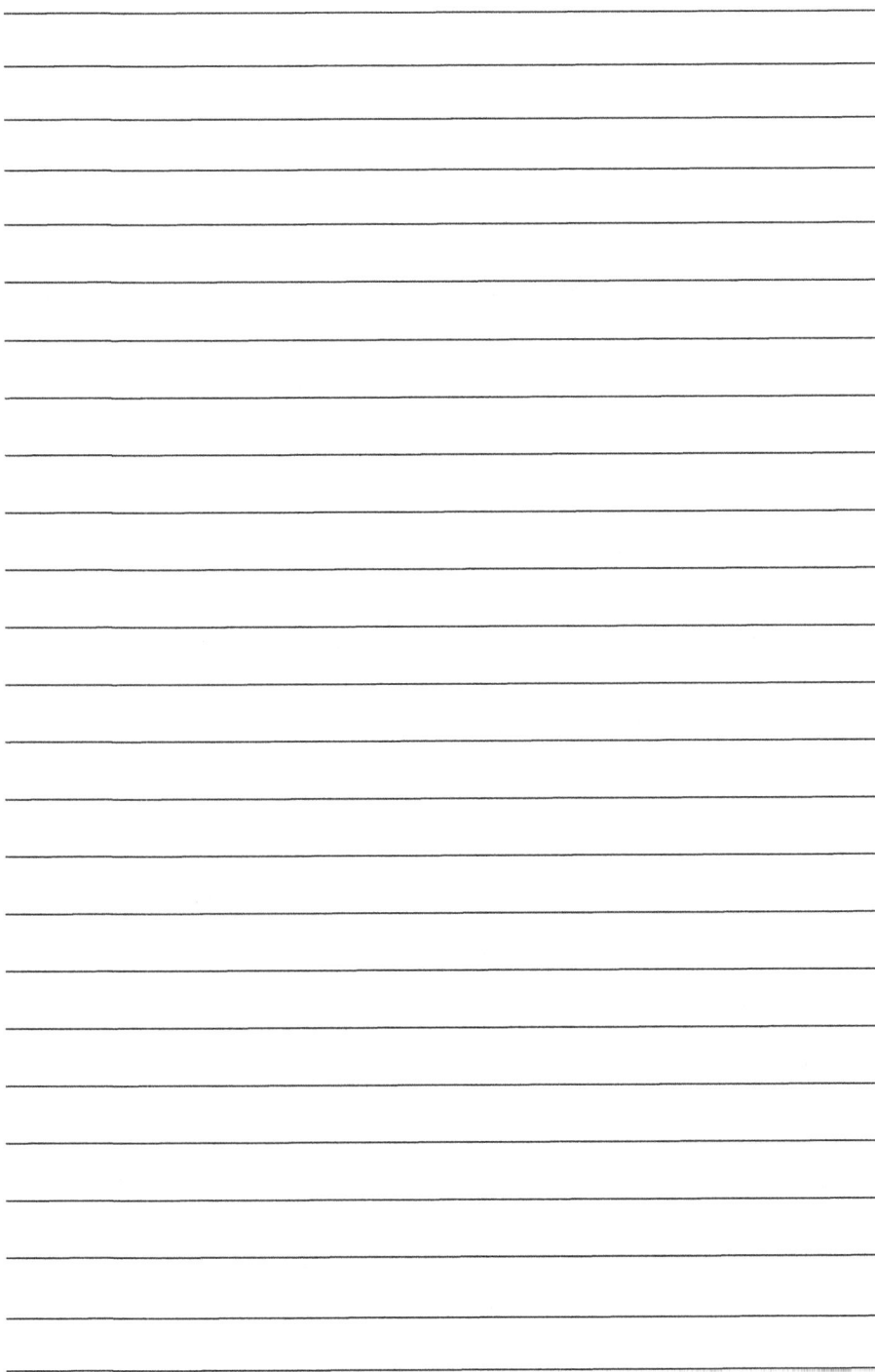

"This is the story of the journey home, and the soul's incessant call for us to recognize the greatness inside ourselves."

-Brandon Bays

_____

_____

_____

_____

_____

_____

_____

_____

_____

_____

_____

_____

_____

_____

_____

_____

_____

_____

_____

_____

_____

_____

_____

_____

_____

_____

_____

_____

o——————————o

"It is good to have an end to journey toward; but it is the journey that matters, in the end."

-Ernest Hemingway

_____

_____

_____

_____

_____

_____

_____

_____

_____

_____

_____

_____

_____

_____

_____

_____

_____

_____

_____

_____

_____

_____

_____

_____

_____

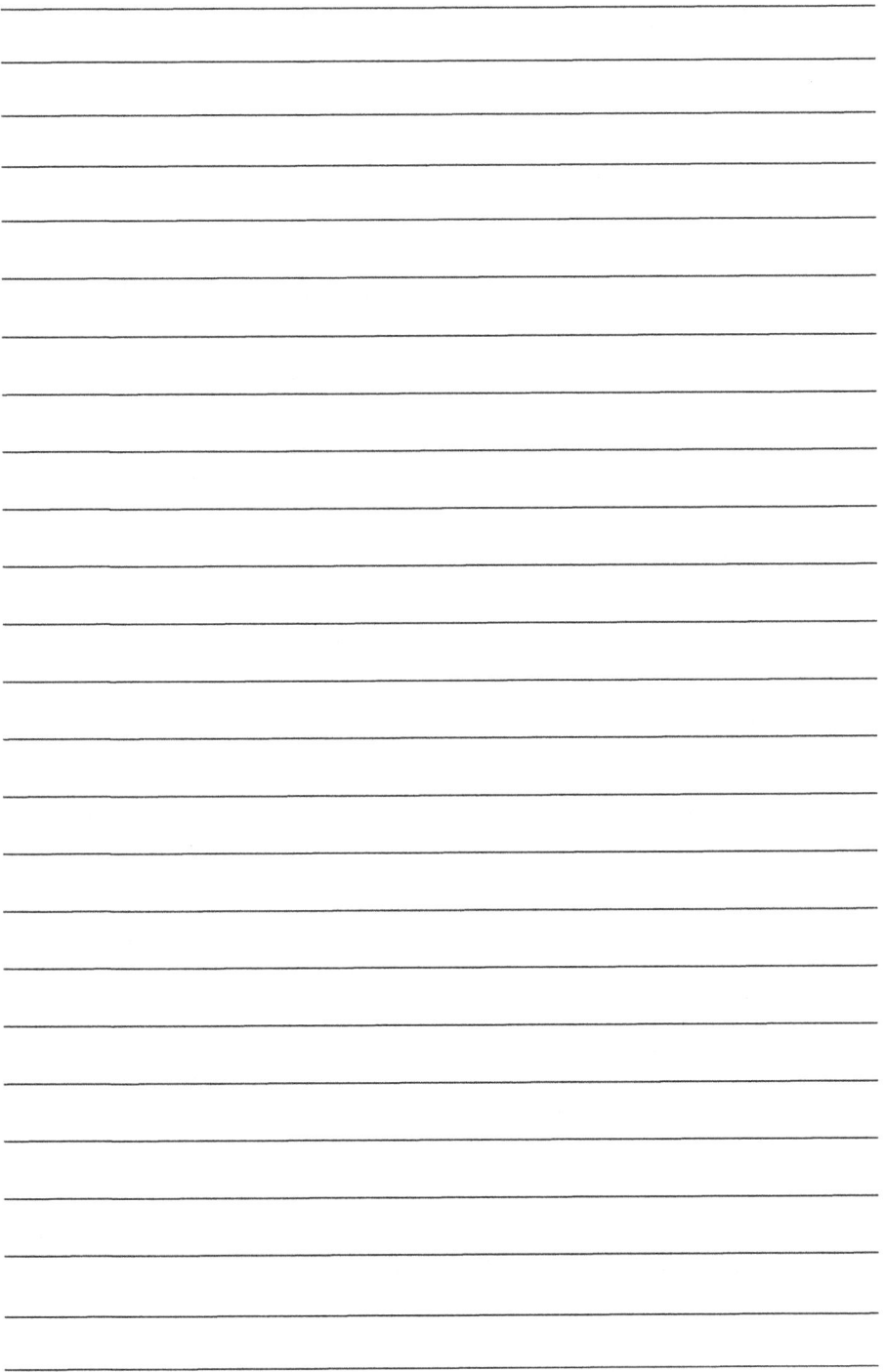

"The main thing that you have to remember on this journey is, just be nice to everyone and always smile."

-Ed Sheeran

_____

_____

_____

_____

_____

_____

_____

_____

_____

_____

_____

_____

_____

_____

_____

_____

_____

_____

_____

_____

_____

_____

_____

_____

o————————o

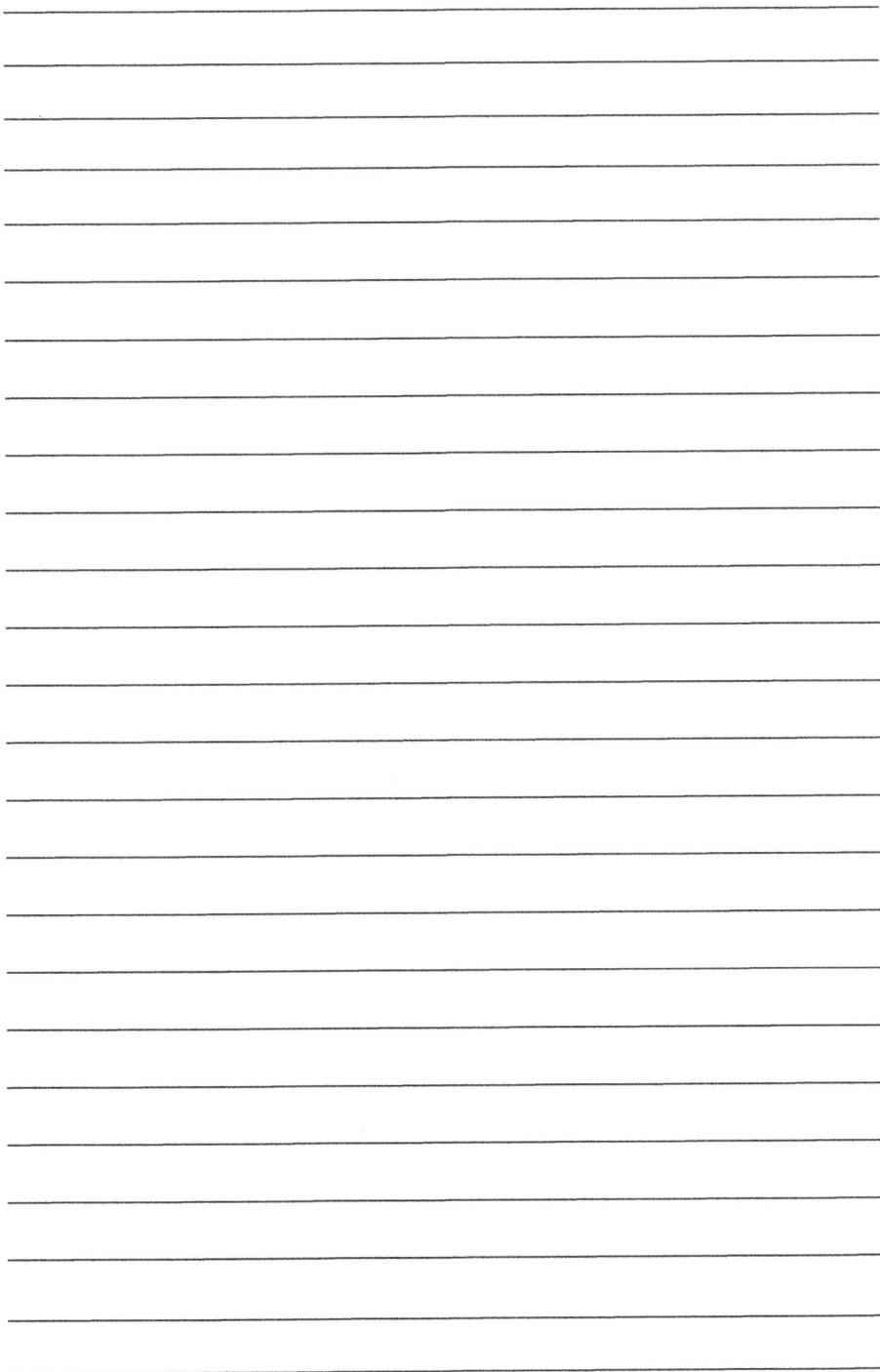

"Do not follow where the path may lead. Go instead where there is no path and leave a trail."

-Ralph Waldo Emerson

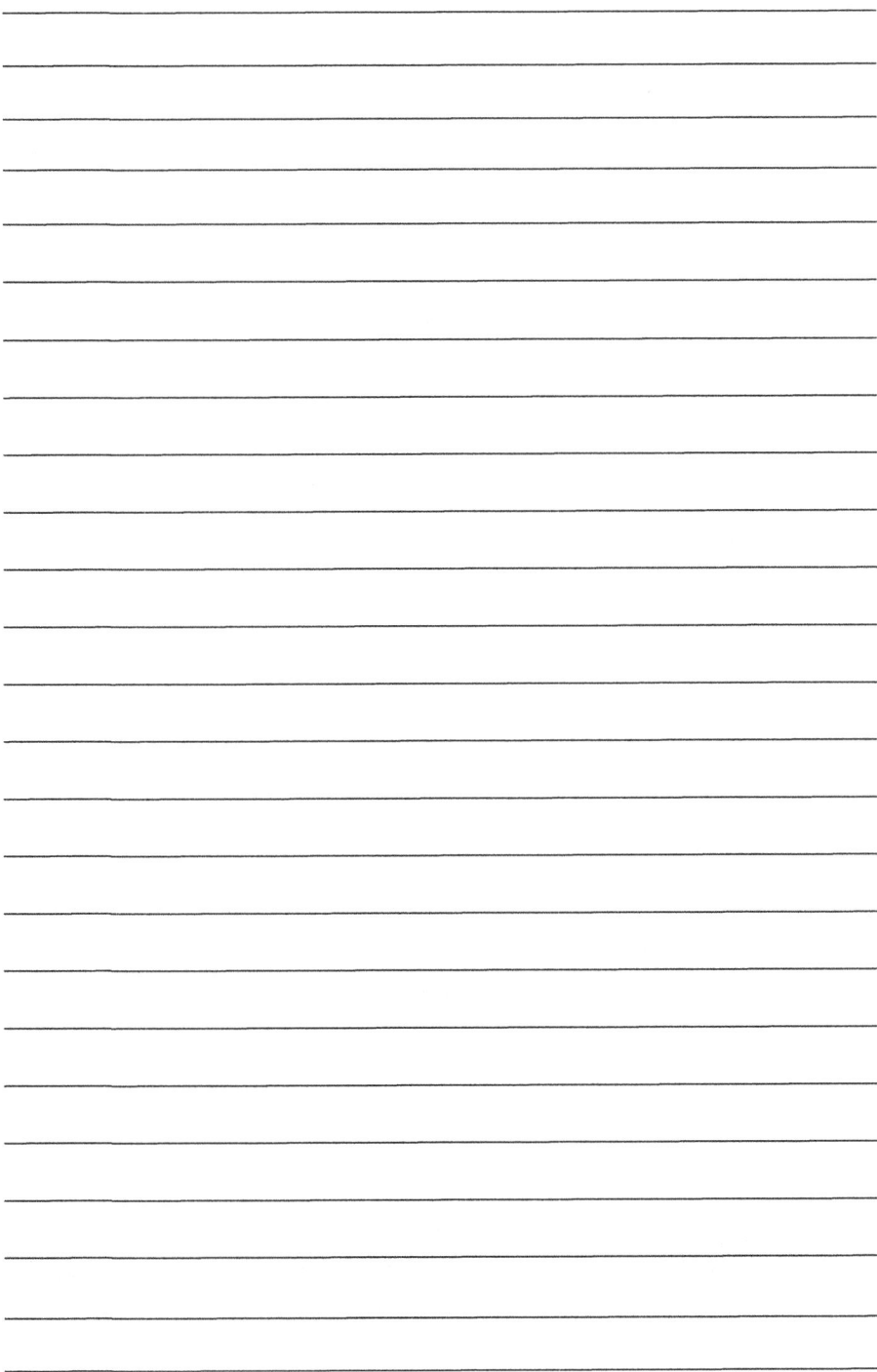

"When you're on a journey and you come to a wall, always throw your pack over first, because then you will be sure to follow."

-Yongey Mingyur Rinpoche

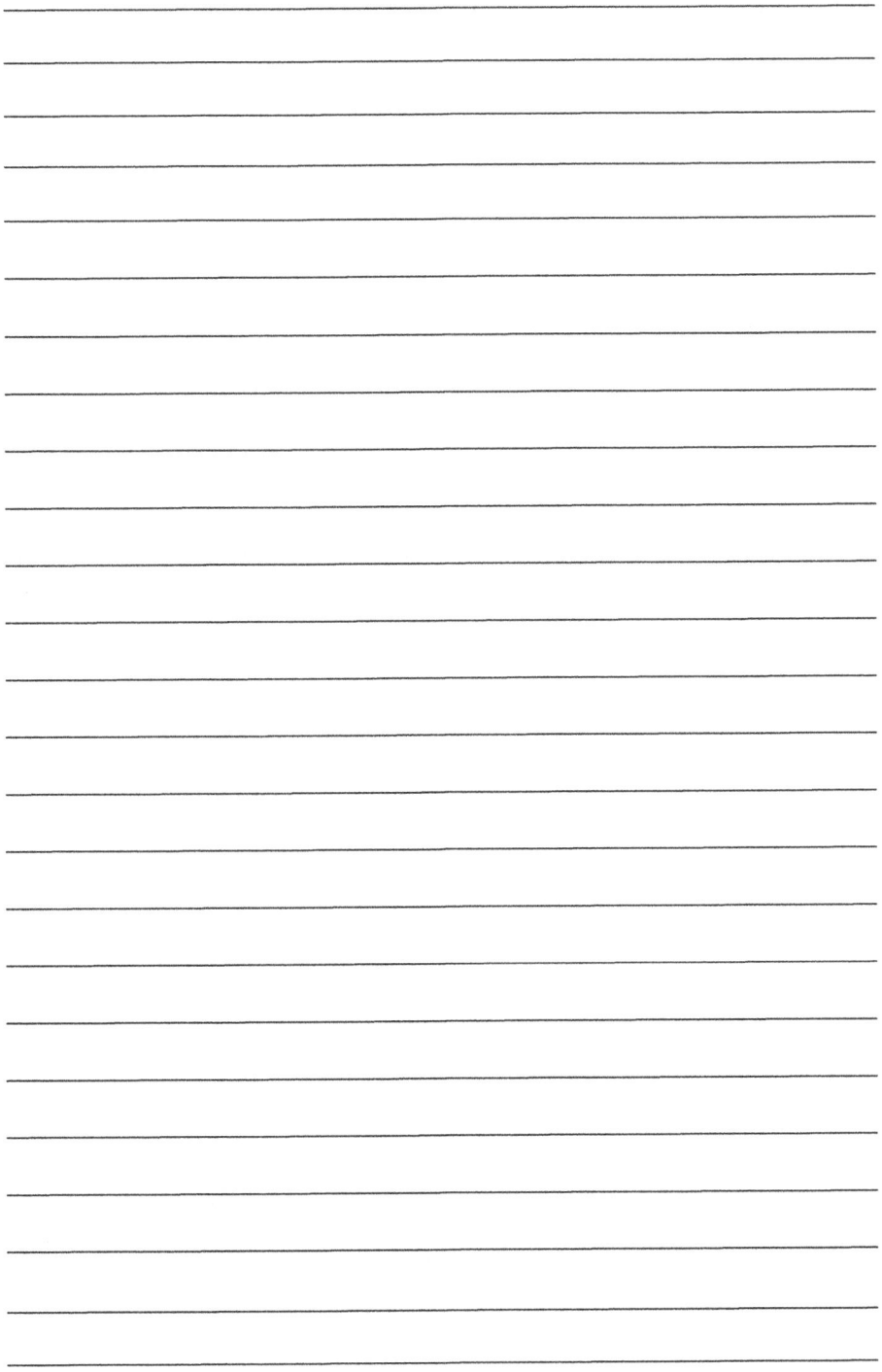

"A journey is best measured in friends rather than miles."

-Tim Cahill

_____

_____

_____

_____

_____

_____

_____

_____

_____

_____

_____

_____

_____

_____

_____

_____

_____

_____

_____

_____

_____

_____

_____

_____

_____

o——————————o

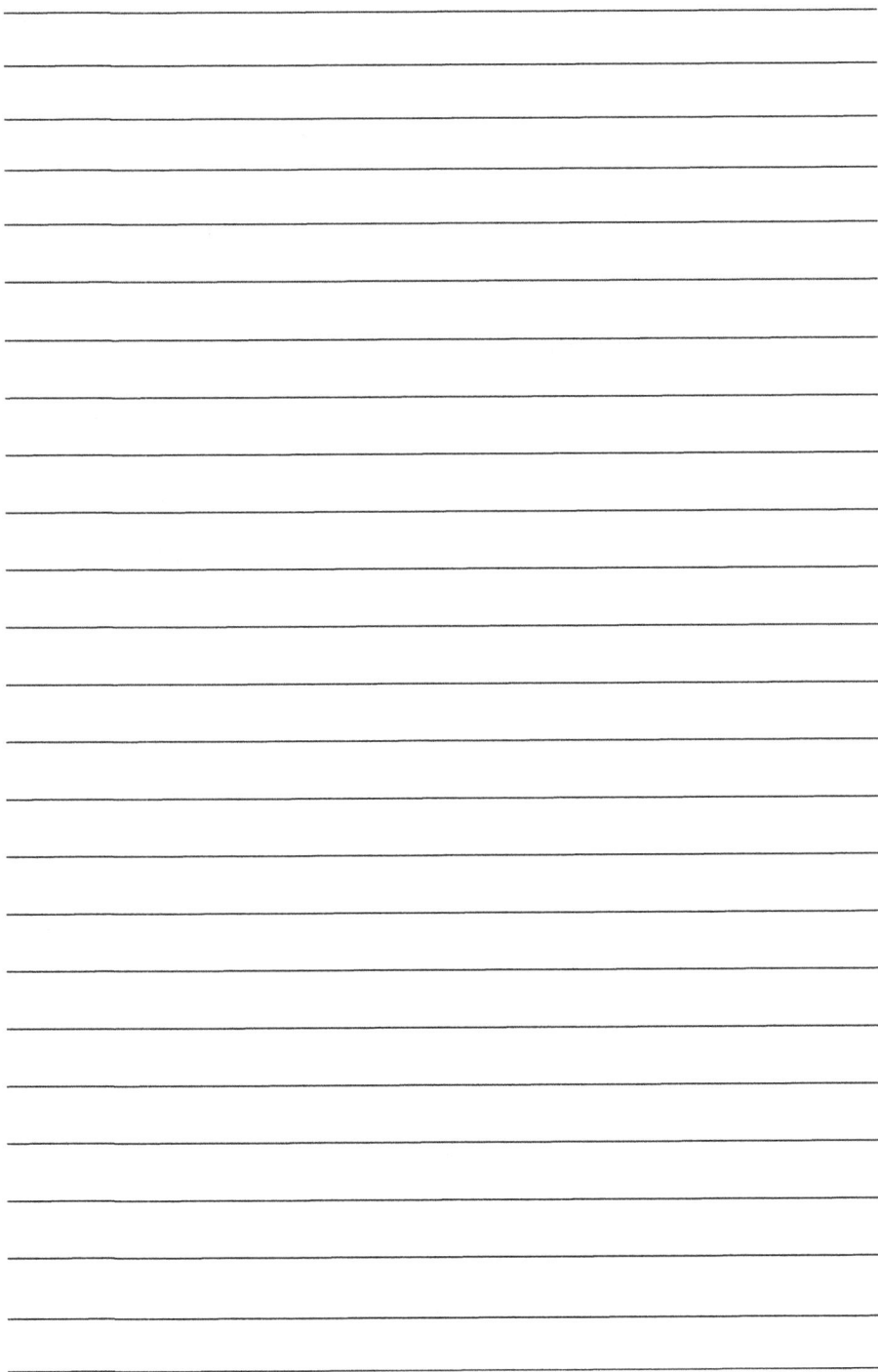

"Not everyone will understand your journey. That's okay. You're here to live your life, not to make everyone understand."

-Banksy

_____

_____

_____

_____

_____

_____

_____

_____

_____

_____

_____

_____

_____

_____

_____

_____

_____

_____

_____

_____

_____

_____

_____

_____

o———————o

"A journey is like marriage. The certain way to be wrong is to think you control it."

-John Steinbeck

_____

_____

_____

_____

_____

_____

_____

_____

_____

_____

_____

_____

_____

_____

_____

_____

_____

_____

_____

_____

_____

_____

_____

_____

_____

_____

o——————o

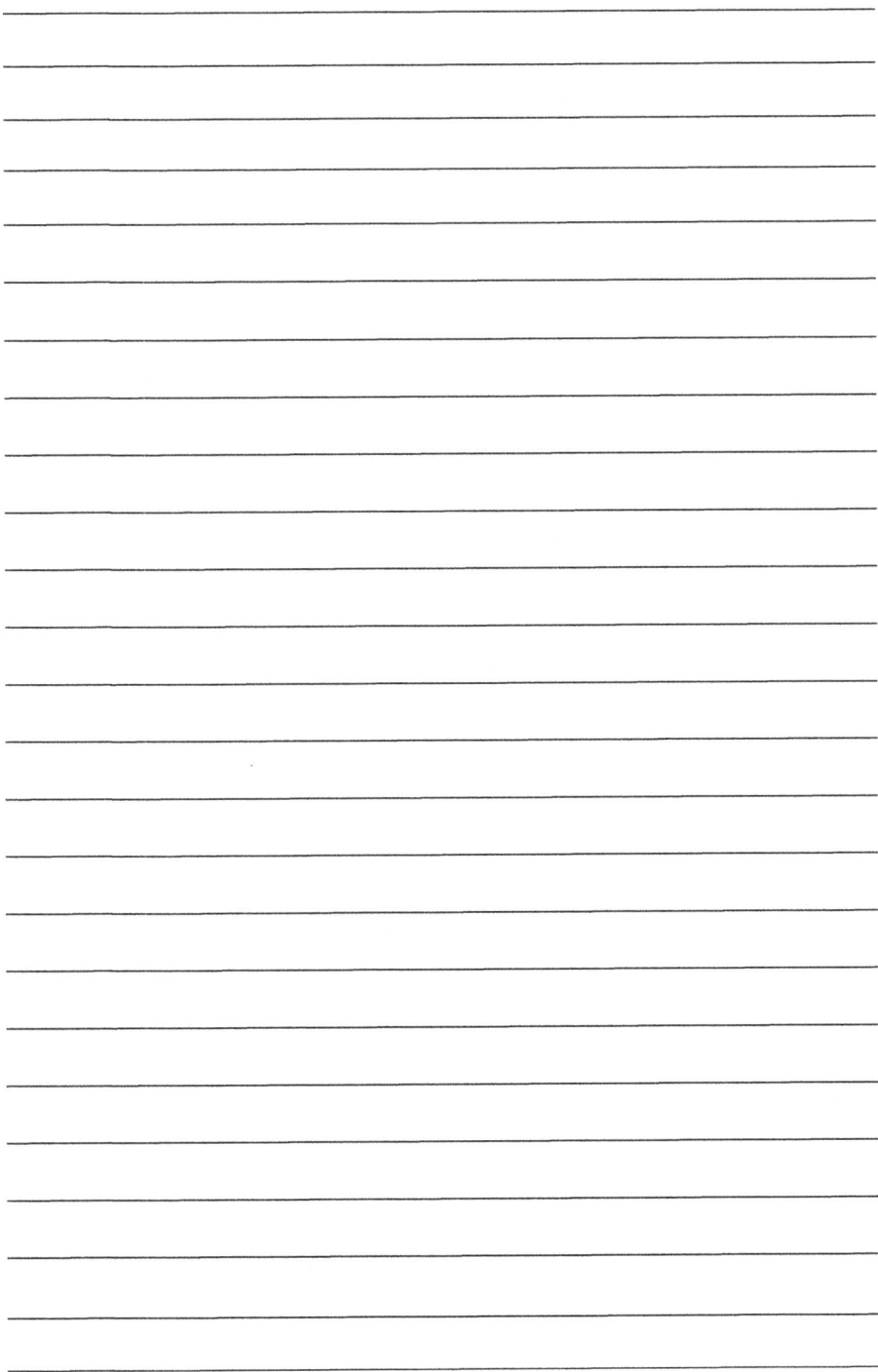

"The hero's journey is not a summit to reach, but a summit that, when you reach it, shows you new summits in front of you waiting to be conquered."

-Victor Hugo Manzanilla

"Make certain of the direction of your thoughts...they can either be destructive or constructive. Both will...lead to a destination...worlds apart from each other."

-Doe Zantamata

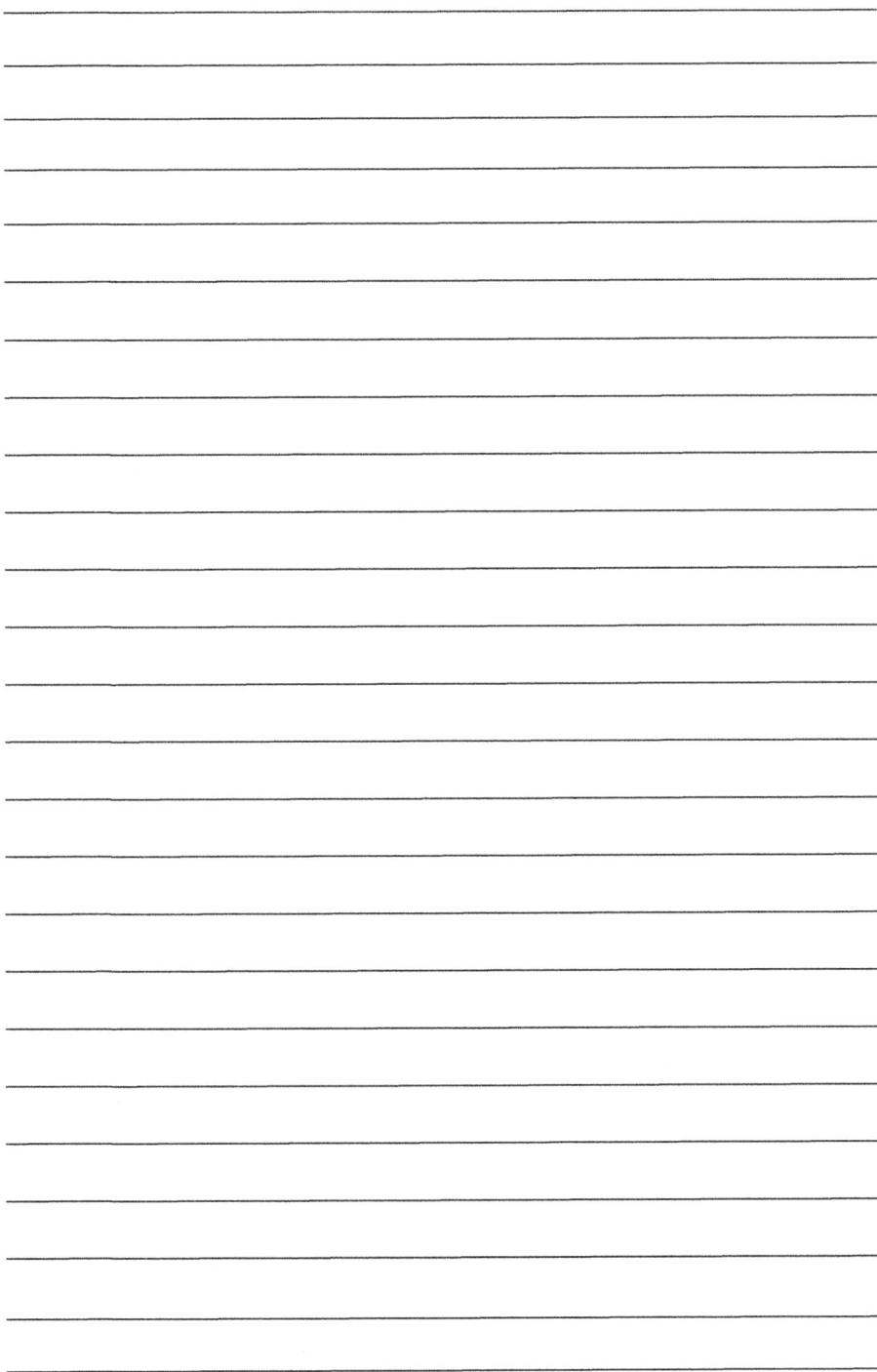

"Take your journey all the way. Don't just do what you want to do. Take all of it and do everything possible to change your life."

-Therese Benedict

Made in the USA
Las Vegas, NV
28 April 2022

48107126R00109